MARK McGWIRE HOME RUN HERO

MARK McGWIRE HOME RUN HERO

ROB RAINS

ST. MARTIN'S PRESS ☙ NEW YORK

ISBN 0-312-20162-1

First Edition: September 1998

10 9 8 7 6 5 4 3 2

CONTENTS

ACKNOWLEDGMENTS

The author wishes to thank everyone who contributed time and effort toward making this book possible, whether researching newspaper articles or making themselves available for an interview or assisting in other ways.

Of particular help were several people from the Oakland A's organization, including Debbie Kenney, Ted Polakowski, Keith Lieppman, Ron Vaughn, Grady Fuson, Dick Bogard, and Karl Kuehl.

Several people who worked with Mark McGwire in the minor leagues contributed stories and interviews, including George Mitterwald, Fred Stanley, and Wendell Kim. Joe McIlvaine and Dick Wiencek provided helpful information about the 1984 draft.

Former USC coach Rod Dedeaux was generous with his time and memory, as were Marcel Lachemann, Art Mazmanian, Jim Dietz, and the staff at the USC sports information office. Former coaches at Damien High School, Tom Carroll and Dick Larson, added their insights to the book, as did childhood friends Scott Larson and Randy Robertson.

Former teammates Walt Weiss and Rick Honeycutt contributed their memories of McGwire, and Ed Randall provided valuable research assistance.

ACKNOWLEDGMENTS

Thanks to the St. Louis Cardinals for their support and cooperation, including Brian Bartow and Walt Jocketty.

The biggest thanks goes to George Witte at St. Martin's Press and to my wife, Sally, and sons, B.J. and Mike, for helping me in more ways than anyone could count.

—ROB RAINS
July 1998

MARK McGWIRE
HOME RUN HERO

1

HOME RUNS DON'T COME EASY

n Mark McGwire's dreams, he is standing at home plate, challenging the record for most home runs hit in a season. The pitcher is on the mound, waiting, ready to throw the ball.

"OK, here it is; try to hit it; let's see if you can do it," McGwire imagines the pitcher saying.

He visualizes the pitch. He visualizes the swing. He can see the bat hitting the ball and taking off . . .

McGwire wakes up, and his fantasy is over. If breaking the home run record is going to happen, it won't be accomplished as easily as a dream suggests. McGwire learned a long time ago that nothing in baseball comes easy, especially home runs.

McGwire thinks hitting a home run might be the hardest thing to do in sports. You can't *try* to hit one, he said, knowing all too well that trying too hard is the first step to failure.

McGwire has established himself as the greatest home run hitter in the major leagues today, so he is a qualified expert on the subject. He also has to face the pressure and expectations that only increase with each homer.

"You get in the box, you see the ball as best you can and react to it and try to hit it," McGwire said. "If it leaves the ballpark, great. If it's a base hit, great. If it's a strikeout, you learn from it. It's not like somebody is putting the ball on the tee for you and saying, 'Here, hit it over the fence.'

"A home run is just a base hit that goes over the fence. Sometimes, if you get a little lift, it goes farther than the one before."

McGwire has always tried to downplay his own importance and accomplishments, but the fact that in consecutive seasons he has been in a position to challenge and perhaps break the record for home runs in a season is testimony to his skills.

He hit 58 homers in 1997 and did so with the combined challenge of changing leagues and teams in midseason and going through a month-long span in which he hit only three homers.

That performance, combined with all of his knowledge of the game, has fortified McGwire with the belief that Roger Maris's mark of 61 homers that has stood since 1961 can be broken. He doesn't say it will be toppled, but it can be.

"If hitting 61 home runs were easy, we wouldn't

be talking about it," McGwire said before the 1998 season began. "Yes, I believe it can be done, but a season has to be absolutely perfect for it to happen. I'm not saying I can do it. I'm not saying I can't. It's not worth talking about until someone goes into September with 50."

McGwire admits he was not a student of baseball history as a youngster and didn't know much about Maris, or Babe Ruth for that matter, until he kept hearing those names in conjunction with his own. That association was first made when he was a rookie with the Oakland A's in 1987, and spent much of the season on a pace to challenge the home run record before finishing the year with the rookie mark of 49.

He knew Ruth was a great home run hitter and one of the greatest players in the history of the game, but that was about the extent of his knowledge.

He knew Maris was the player who broke Ruth's 1927 record of 60 homers, and that he played most of his career in the shadow of Mickey Mantle, but not much else.

He didn't know that when Maris was chasing Ruth in 1961 his hair began to fall out, in clumps. He didn't know how almost everybody, including those within the Yankee organization, rooted against Maris. He wasn't the fair-haired boy; he wasn't the hand-picked successor to the throne. Mantle, after Joe DiMaggio, was the golden boy. Had Mantle gone into the final week of the season with 59 homers, people would have been cheering him on, not hoping he failed.

Maris broke the record, but he never got the thrill of being recognized for it. The commissioner of baseball at the time, Ford Frick, put an asterisk behind the number 61 and made baseball recognize both Maris's achievement and Ruth's mark of 60, because it had been established in a 154-game season rather than Maris's 162-game season.

Once Maris had finally broken through the 60-homer barrier that had stood for 33 years, people thought it would happen more often, as had been the case when Roger Bannister finally broke the four-minute barrier for the mile run. Once Maris established the possibility that it could happen, others surely would follow.

None has, at least until now, when McGwire, Ken Griffey Jr., and Sammy Sosa all spent the first half of the 1998 season on a pace to break Maris's record.

Maris, perhaps worn out by the struggle to get the record, never enjoyed it. He died of cancer in 1985 at the too-young age of 51. His family, however, has watched possible challengers come and go and seen the mark continue to stand. They are perhaps the only ones rooting against McGwire and the other challengers.

"The family would like to see the record last forever," Maris's brother, Rudy, told *New York Newsday* as the end of the 1997 season approached. "It's kind of exciting that the record is being challenged every year. It's creating interest, and I guess that's good."

Maris had one golden season in an otherwise unremarkable career. His previous career best was 39 homers in 1960. He hit 33 in 1962, and that was the most he hit in a season for the rest of his career.

"Maris was never comfortable with New York," columnist Steve Jacobson of *New York Newsday* wrote in 1997. "Yankee tradition was Ruth, DiMaggio, and Mantle. Maris was the outsider; he felt the Yankees wanted Mantle to be the one to break the record. He may have been right, but they didn't hinder him. He didn't forgive them.

"He and Mantle shared an apartment; they got along, but Maris resented the establishment. He resented the Yankees for questioning his intention when doctors couldn't find the broken bone in his hand in 1963. He never hit more than 33 homers again."

Dave Anderson, a Pulitzer Prize–winning columnist for *The New York Times*, said McGwire, Griffey, or anybody else challenging the record today will face more media pressure than Maris did, but the other demands will be less strenuous.

"That was a hellish experience for Roger," Anderson once said, "something that went way beyond the media. The aura of Ruth was overwhelming. You know the story about Maris losing some of his hair during that time; it was falling out of his head from stress. Just to give you some idea, even the commissioner of baseball didn't want Ruth's record to fall. Ford Frick, the guy who wanted an asterisk attached to Maris's record, had once been a ghostwriter for Ruth."

Maris had to deal with reporters from 10 New York area newspapers, including seven from metropolitan New York. There was no CNN, ESPN, or all-sports radio stations to hound him every step of the way. McGwire or whoever is closest to the record in September, will have to put dealing with the media right behind facing the opposing pitcher as the most difficult obstacle toward breaking the record.

Early in his career, McGwire was teammates with Jose Canseco and predicted that if either of them was going to mount a challenge to Maris's mark, Canseco would be the one to do it.

"If either of us ever hits 60 homers, it will be Jose," McGwire said in 1988. "He's just so strong. It's out of this world."

Most observers now make those comments about McGwire, who has hit the longest measured home runs at seven major-league stadiums—Busch Stadium in St. Louis, Comiskey Park in Chicago, Jacobs Field in Cleveland, the Kingdome in Seattle, the Metrodome in Minneapolis, Skydome in Toronto, and Tiger Stadium in Detroit.

That isn't a fact McGwire would be able to repeat off the top of his head. He doesn't keep mental notes that verify his own accomplishments, just as he doesn't keep physical reminders around either. His Rookie of the Year award from 1987 is locked away in a storage facility in California with other memorabilia. His Gold Glove is on display at his optometrist's office. One of his two Silver Sluggers awards was given to his father.

Where would he put an award for hitting the most homers in a season? Don't ask.

It took McGwire a long time to figure out that he is a home run hitter, one with the best home run to at-bat ratio in major-league history. He entered the 1998 season second to Ruth but passed him with an electrifying April and May. McGwire doesn't need a trophy or a plaque to remind him of his place in history. That will have to fall to others to decide.

"God gives you something at birth, and you are on this earth to try to figure out what it is," McGwire said. "It's not to copy somebody's swing or jump shot or the way he passes the football. You have to be yourself. So many children today try not being themselves, and that's why they get in trouble.

"When they don't succeed trying to be somebody else, then they walk away from the game. They say, 'I'm not any good.' How do they know?"

McGwire said he played with other youths in high school who had just as much talent and baseball ability as he did. He knows that they think the only reason McGwire made it to the majors, and they didn't, was luck.

"I'm sure they are sitting on their couch at home now saying they could have made it," McGwire said. "You know what stopped them? Themselves. That's what stops kids today. Nobody stops them but themselves."

Failure is a great teacher, and McGwire has seen a lot of failure in baseball. He has failed, but he has grown from the experience. It has made his mind stronger, and he has come to the realization that it's the most important piece of equipment in a player's possession.

"My mind is very strong," McGwire said in June 1998. "I'm very in tune with what the pitcher has. I'm very in tune to the situation I'll be in during a given at-bat.

"The mind is the strongest thing on your body. And if you tell your mind you're going to fail, you're going to fail. But if you're putting so much positive reinforcement in there, it's going to give you a better chance to do something that given day."

McGwire has never been someone who said "what if." He doesn't live in the past, preferring to look to the future.

"I don't think you succeed in life or sports if you sit back and say, 'What if I did this?'" McGwire said. "You can't go back and get those days. I'm a firm believer that people who live in the past never succeed in anything. They're always failing."

McGwire is worried about one aspect of chasing the record. He could miss it and still become the first person in history to hit 50 or more homers in three consecutive seasons. Nobody has ever done that in the major leagues, not even Ruth.

"Is that failure, because I didn't get to 60 or 61?" McGwire asked. "That's the thing I'm afraid of. If it doesn't happen, and there's that chance, and because it's so built up right now, how is the media going to take that? . . . What if I don't do it? Are people going to write that I failed?"

That thought passes after a moment, and won't return to McGwire's mind anytime soon. He won't let it. Ever since his days growing up playing with friends at the end of a cul-de-sac in Claremont, California, McGwire has been in control of his own fate, just as he is now.

He wouldn't have it any other way.

2

CHILDHOOD

For countless youngsters, growing up to become a professional athlete is the only thing they dream about. They identify with a player and/or a team and have visions that someday they will be playing in the major leagues or the NFL alongside their hero.

Only a tiny handful of kids ever get to realize those dreams. Some players who do eventually rise to the major leagues and become stars say they were too busy playing the game as youngsters to ever think that far into the future.

McGwire was one of those kids. Growing up in a middle-class athletic family in Claremont, California, McGwire was one of five boys, all of whom were involved in whatever sport was in season. He said the first time he seriously thought he might be able to

10

make a career out of baseball was when he was a junior in high school and began attracting the attention of pro scouts in the area.

McGwire's earliest sporting memories are of golf and going out on the course to caddy for his father, John, when he was only five years old.

"Golf was the first game I learned," McGwire said. "My dad taught me how to grip a club when I was five, and I never had another lesson."

McGwire and his brothers all became very good golfers, and when he was a sophomore in high school McGwire actually quit the baseball team to concentrate on golf.

"I had pulled a chest muscle, so it would be a while before I could really swing a bat," he said. "I had been playing on the junior varsity team, which didn't excite me much. I'd been playing golf for years. My dad used to take me to the peewee courses when I was six or seven, and I'd developed my own swing. I never had a lesson."

McGwire still remembers playing in a tournament at age 15, when he shot a personal-best round of 72 to tie him for the lead and put him into a sudden-death play-off. McGwire and his opponent remained tied through the first four extra holes, before McGwire finally sank a birdie putt on the fifth play-off hole to earn his first victory.

"The thing I liked about golf was that you were the only one there to blame when something went wrong," said McGwire, who lowered his handicap to 4 by playing so much. "I missed baseball, though, and I went back to it."

McGwire did keep up with golf and played in several pro-am tournaments as a celebrity after he reached the major leagues. Performing in front of those crowds created a different kind of pressure, he said.

"The weirdest and probably the scariest thing that I've ever done was at the first practice round I ever played for the AT&T at Pebble Beach," McGwire said. "There might have been 50 people watching. I got up to the tee and I was nervous as hell. What did I do but look up and hit it right to the ladies' tee. How embarrassing. It was something I'll never forget. It was the first time I ever had that feeling."

McGwire began playing youth baseball when he was eight years old. A neighbor was on the team and asked McGwire if he wanted to join him. McGwire had been playing soccer, which at the time was a more popular sport in Claremont, but thought baseball sounded fun as well.

"We grew up on this great cul-de-sac," McGwire said. "We got broken pieces of drywall from the homes being built nearby and marked off a football field with it like chalk. We played with a Nerf ball in the street and we played baseball there with a tennis ball."

Numerous newspaper and magazine stories have been written over the years detailing how McGwire hit a home run over the right field fence in his first Little League at-bat. While the stories technically are true, they are a little misleading. McGwire did homer in his first "official" Little League at-bat, when he was

10 years old. But the homer came after he had been playing in a different youth league for a couple of years.

Because he was taller and stronger than most kids his age, McGwire's natural athletic ability separated him from most of the other youngsters. He pitched for most of his Little League career for the Claremont LL Athletics, and his father can't recall McGwire's team ever losing a regular-season game when McGwire was on the mound. When he wasn't pitching, he played shortstop. He batted cleanup.

Several observers stopped McGwire's parents to remark on their son's baseball skills and predicted that he would one day become a star in the major leagues.

"As parents, we never gloated over Mark's success," John McGwire said in an interview in 1990 with the Inland, California, *Empire Magazine*. "Even when some of the city's old-time ballplayers and opposing Little League coaches would stop and tell me that Mark was a future big leaguer, I never let him know about it."

McGwire's parents, however, had one major concern about their son and any potential success he might have in sports: his eyesight. McGwire himself says, "I have the worst eyes you could possibly have. No lie. Without contacts or glasses, I can't even see the big *E* on the eye chart."

The McGwires noticed that Mark was having problems seeing when he began sitting too close to the television, saying it was the only way he could make out the picture. One time when he was eight, McGwire ran into a wild streak while pitching and, after he walked too many batters, his father—who was his coach—moved him to shortstop. McGwire said the view from that distance was fuzzy, and when his parents had his eyes checked shortly thereafter they learned he needed glasses.

McGwire wore glasses until he was a freshman in high school, when he became one of the first kids in his neighborhood to begin wearing contact lenses.

Years later, after he reached the majors, a friend once asked McGwire if he was nearsighted or far-sighted. McGwire answered, "Blind."

His optometrist in Oakland, Stephen Johnson, said the correct diagnosis was that McGwire was "extremely nearsighted, with an awful lot of astigmatism. That gets real, real tricky."

Dr. Johnson said the vision is correctable, with the proper lens, to 20–10. For years McGwire has done eye exercises to try to get the optimal eyesight possible. He went through approximately 40 different kinds of lenses before 1990, when Johnson fitted him with what he thought were the best lenses for McGwire.

Wearing contacts didn't solve all of McGwire's problems as a youngster. One of his childhood friends, Scott Larson, recalled the time they were playing for Damien High School in a basketball game and one of McGwire's contacts fell out.

"We had to stop the game to look for it." Larson said. "I don't remember if we found it or not."

Larson became friends with McGwire in seventh grade, when he moved to the area. McGwire and some of the kids already living in Claremont and attending La Puerta Middle School quickly accepted Larson into their group.

"As a new kid it was nice to have guys take you under their arm," Larson said. "McGwire was a popular kid. My brother Todd and he played on the same Little League team, and even then he was hitting home runs that astounded everybody. He could throw hard, and he was always such a pure hitter. He always had the same swing."

Larson and the other kids in the neighborhood knew McGwire was a big, strong kid and a good athlete, but none of them predicted a future successful professional baseball career. They were too busy being kids and called McGwire by his nickname at the time—Tree—because of his size and red hair, and also a reference to the redwoods Northern California is known for.

"We played every sport there was," Larson said. "We didn't grow up in a spirit of parents pushing their kids to be professional athletes. We were all just having fun. I never thought that one day he was going to be in the big leagues.

"Being so tall opened a lot of doors for Mark, but he was never the type of guy who would bully people around. Even when he was 6-foot-5 in high school, he had problems slam-dunking a basketball."

McGwire said the difference between when he was a child and today is the increased pressure many parents place on their children to try to become a successful athlete, knowing what the financial rewards could mean.

"People lose perspective because of the salaries we make," McGwire said. "There are parents pushing their kids into this so they can someday make all this money. But that's not realistic and it's not what it's all about. It should be about having fun and your friends."

Another kid from the neighborhood, Randy Robertson, grew up with McGwire and Larson, went on to play baseball with McGwire in college, and spent two and a half years as a pitcher in the Padres organization.

"He really was kind of a gentle giant," Robertson said of McGwire. "All the kids always were playing jokes on him because he got scared so easily."

One incident Robertson recalled occurred when the boys were about sixteen and were alone at McGwire's house, watching television.

"We kept hearing a noise upstairs," Robertson said. "We didn't think it was anything, and I went home. About a half hour later, he called me and was scared and said, 'Somebody's in the house.' My dad came with me and went over there, and when we pulled in the driveway, the garage door was open and Mark was standing there with a pair of scissors in his hand. He pointed in the garage and said, 'They're in there. They're trapped in there.'

"My dad had his headlights on and he told whoever it was to come out. It turned out it was two friends of ours who knew Mark was there alone, and they were throwing pebbles on the roof to try to scare him. It worked."

Larson recalls the neighborhood kids spending much of their free time at the McGwires' house. With five boys, it always was the center of activity.

"It was obvious he came from a house with no girls, because he would always be sitting around in his underwear watching TV and he wouldn't get up and change when you came over," Robertson said. "Whenever you went over there you never knocked; you just walked in the door like you lived there, too."

The kids chose to hang out there because they had a great deal of respect for McGwire's parents, John and Ginger McGwire.

"His parents are incredible people who are a big part of the community," Larson said. "They were an influential family, and always went out of their way to do the right thing to help kids."

McGwire's parents met in Seattle, when John McGwire was a dentistry student at the University of Washington. Ginger was working as a nurse for two of John's professors, who also maintained off-campus practices.

When he was a boy, seven years old, John McGwire was stricken with polio. He was forced to spend several months in bed, and the illness left one of his legs shorter than the other, forcing him to walk with a cane. The illness limited McGwire's ability to play sports, but he developed a love of golf that he passed on to his sons, as well as interest in all other sports.

Ginger McGwire had participated in numerous sports growing up, including golf, tennis, skiing, volleyball, and basketball. While in high school she won several medals in swimming at a Seattle athletic club.

John McGwire later became interested in bicycling and once pedaled 400 miles between San Francisco and Santa Barbara as part of a camping trip. He also trained as an amateur boxer and continued to pound away on the speed bag in the garage as Mark and his four brothers were growing up.

Mike McGwire was the oldest of the boys, and he became an Eagle Scout at age 14. He played varsity soccer and golf at Claremont High School. After Mark, next in line was Bobby McGwire, who went to Damien with Mark and was a first-string soccer player and one of the top performers on the school's golf team.

The football star of the family was Dan McGwire, the tallest of the McGwire boys at 6-foot-8, who guided Claremont High to a 36–3–1 record during his years as the team's starting quarterback, passing for 65 touchdowns. He was heavily recruited out of high school and accepted a scholarship offer from the University of Iowa because he liked their pass-oriented offense, and he dreamed of one day returning to Southern California to play in the Rose Bowl.

Those dreams didn't materialize, however, as Dan McGwire and Iowa coach Hayden Fry couldn't agree on McGwire's role with the team and he transferred to San Diego State. He did become a first-round draft pick of the Seattle Seahawks but failed to become a star in the NFL.

McGwire's youngest brother, J. J., was a defensive tackle at Claremont before turning his attention to competitive weight lifting and bodybuilding while in college, after suffering an eye injury.

None of McGwire's brothers chose to play baseball past high school, but their parents wanted *them* to make those decisions and never forced any of their sons to play one sport or another.

Most of the people who watch McGwire now don't believe that he never played football in high school or at any other level.

McGwire's opinion, then and now, was that he didn't want to spend four or five nights a week practicing and only play one game a week. "I thought it was a waste of time," McGwire said.

Only once did the football coach at Damien, Dick Larson—the father of McGwire's friend Scott Larson—ask McGwire about coming out for the team.

"He just didn't want to play," said Larson, who also had McGwire in English class at Damien, a private all-boys Catholic school of about eight hundred students. "If a kid really didn't want to play, I stayed out of it. He could have been a variety of things, which is why I never browbeat him about participating."

Larson remembers McGwire as "very much a regular kid, well liked by other students and not regarded as a star athlete. He had a solid base in his family and was just a very solid citizen."

About the only incident Larson recalled McGwire ever being involved in was when his son Scott and McGwire were with several other friends at McGwire's house.

"We had a little trick we did with gasoline," Scott Larson said. "We would put a little in a Dixie cup, light it, and then throw the cup. It looked like the fire was flying through the air.

"This time we had a friend who hadn't seen the trick, and when we went to show him, I was standing in back and the cup accidentally flew into my face and caught my face on fire. I was in shock, and we all ran into the house and looked in the mirror and started crying.

"Mark was so upset and scared. He thought his parents were going to kill him. I was wearing a new jacket of his brother's that Mark had borrowed and it had gotten burned, too."

The kids were afraid to tell their parents what actually had happened, so they made up a story about an accident with a minibike. It wasn't until years later that both families learned what actually happened.

Fortunately, Larson's wounds healed and did not leave any scars, only memories.

Tom Carroll, the baseball coach and athletic director at Damien, has many memories of McGwire. Carroll's fondest memory has nothing to do with baseball but recalls the type of young man McGwire was, treating people with respect and being well mannered and never causing any problems.

"I really enjoyed him when he was here," Carroll said. "If anything, I would say he had a tendency to be a little on the shy side. He never wanted to be the guy out front, which he could have been. If he had been from Pittsburgh you would have said he was a blue-collar guy because that was his approach.

"What separated him from other kids was his work ethic. You've got to have talent to make it, but there are a lot of kids with talent who don't work at it. Mark was never afraid to work extra. The basic tools were all there for him to be a success."

Carroll does have memories of McGwire from the baseball field, such as the time Damien was playing a game at Ganesha High School in Pomona. The school is adjacent to the 10 Freeway and built on a slope, which creates a wind tunnel in the outfield. "The wind just knocked anything hit up in the air straight down," Carroll said.

That wasn't the case on this particular day. McGwire hit a ball that not only cleared a 60-foot fence, built to protect the nearby houses, but landed on the street in front of the house. The last thing Carroll saw was the ball bouncing down the street.

"He must have hit it above the wind," Carroll said. "It was a tremendous blast, and Ganesha's coach told me he had been there for something like 16 or 17 years and had never seen a ball hit that far either."

The other long ball that Carroll remembers was foul, but still impressive. Playing at Damien, McGwire hit a ball that cleared the 320-foot fence, went across a soccer field, and bounced on one hop through an open door into the school gym.

"It sounds like one of those made-up stories, but I know it's true," Carroll said.

Robertson remembers two games from high school. He went to Claremont, the public high school in town that McGwire attended as a freshman before transferring to Damien. They were opponents in those games but played together in Legion ball. That's when McGwire once hit a ball—literally—into the next county.

"We were playing a game in Upland, in Los Angeles County, and behind the left field fence was a street," Robertson said. "On the other side of the street was the county line for San Bernardino County. Mark hit one over the fence and across the street, so he did literally hit the ball into another county."

During a Legion tournament in Laramie, Wyoming, McGwire was set to pitch the championship game and was warming up for the game in the bullpen when Robertson's father walked behind the bench of the other team. Those kids were mesmerized watching McGwire, because he was such a big kid and was popping the ball into the catcher's mitt.

"My dad said, 'Are you looking at that pitcher? He throws hard, but he's so wild. He's got no idea where it's going. He hit three guys the last time he pitched.' All Mark had to do was throw fastballs down the middle and he blew it right by those guys. He pitched a no-hitter and we won the tournament."

One of Robertson's proudest moments in his rivalry/friendship with McGwire came during a junior varsity game when Robertson struck out McGwire in four consecutive at-bats.

"He still was not a disciplined hitter then, and if you didn't throw him a strike you were OK," Robertson said. "As he got older he learned the strike zone and got more disciplined."

Like most boys, McGwire and his friends enjoyed going to as many major-league games as possible. The California Angels, playing in Anaheim, were the closest team, but McGwire said he was never particularly a fan of the team or of any particular player.

"I'm glad I didn't pay any attention to players when I was a kid," McGwire said. "Today kids pay too much attention to what big-league players are like and they want to be like them instead of being themselves. The first and foremost thing is you can only do what God gave you. God didn't give you the ability to copy somebody. He gave you the ability to swing a bat or throw a pitch in your own style."

It was McGwire's own ability, even at an early age, that convinced his father that Mark had a chance to become a professional baseball player.

"The surprising thing was he had an innate sense of how to play," the elder McGwire said. "He knew where to position players; he just knew. It was spine-tingling, his understanding of the game at such an early age."

When McGwire was 14, his parents enrolled him in a summer baseball clinic for kids at Cal Poly Pomona, directed by John Scolinos, the school's head coach, who had a reputation for taking kids with a lot of raw talent and developing them into polished players.

Scolinos saw a special talent in McGwire.

"The kid was a natural," Scolinos said. "I had him throw for me in the bullpen. Except for a couple of minor adjustments we made in his mechanics, he already knew how to pitch."

Receiving any kind of special attention, even at an early age, made McGwire uncomfortable.

"I was always the kind of kid who liked to sit in the back of the room and just blend in," McGwire said in a 1988 interview with *Sports Illustrated*. "I was always just a basic athlete, nothing extraordinary. But I was a hard worker. And I liked to do a lot of that work where people couldn't see me. I'd throw balls against a cement wall or set a ball on a tee and hit it."

That even had something to do with getting a perm and growing an Afro while in junior high, Robertson said.

"He kind of looked like Bozo the clown," Robertson said. "He had all that red hair tied up in a big 'fro. It was kind of the style then; a few other kids had one. I think he kept it about six months."

If his friends were involved in something, McGwire was more interested in participating, especially if he wasn't expected to be the star. He was the starting center on the Damien basketball team for two years, but the principal reason he played was to hang out with his friends.

Said Carroll, "He didn't paint his hair green or do anything outrageous that would be more exciting. It sounds boring today, but he was the kind of kid you never had to worry about. I give a lot of credit to his parents, who raised all of their kids to be great kids."

After he had become a rookie sensation with the Oakland Athletics in 1987, McGwire's mother, Ginger, told the *Christian Science Monitor*, "I've never felt that Mark was ever as impressed with his success in sports as other people. Aware of it, yes, but never big-headed about it. I've always assumed that we were like most families—that we tried to teach our kids the importance of always doing their best, being polite and respecting other people."

When he was in high school, McGwire thought he might like to become a police officer if he didn't go into baseball. It was one of the things he thought about sitting in the back of the classroom, when he wasn't trying to perfect his autograph.

"When I was bored, which was many days, I used to sit in the back of the class and practice my signature," McGwire said. "Sometimes when I turned in my paperwork the teacher would have no idea who this person was because I wouldn't print my name."

McGwire has since modified his autograph, but it still is hard to read—something he doesn't spend much time worrying about.

Whether he was going to go to college—and where—or whether he would immediately pursue a baseball career didn't worry McGwire much either.

As a senior at Damien, McGwire led the team with a .359 average and five homers. On the mound, he was 5–3 with a glittering ERA of 1.90, good enough to earn second-team All-California Interscholastic Federation honors. He was noticed by some college coaches, including Ben Hines, at the time an assistant coach at Arizona State.

Hines saw McGwire play in a tournament and told his father the school was interested in offering Mark a scholarship.

"Hines said he'd like me to fly to Tempe to visit the campus, and promised to contact me with the details," McGwire said. "After a week or so, I still hadn't heard from him, so my dad called ASU and the trip was arranged. I went to Tempe, enjoyed myself, and was told they were still interested in me and would give me a call soon."

Before anyone from ASU got back to McGwire, he heard from the coaching staff at the University of Southern California. They were interested in him as well.

Art Mazmanian was the baseball coach at Mount San Antonio Junior College in Walnut, California, and his district had 24 high schools, including Damien. He had seen McGwire play on a couple of occasions and knew he was a Division I talent. An alumnus of USC, Mazmanian tipped off head coach Rod Dedeaux and his pitching coach at the time, Marcel Lachemann.

Lachemann had pitched for Mazmanian when he was in high school, and the two had maintained a good relationship. "I told Lachemann he was the kind of kid you didn't need to see more than once to be impressed," Mazmanian said.

Lachemann watched McGwire pitch three times and saw a pitcher with a good fastball, in the high eighties, and sound command of all of his pitches. With refinement and more experience, Lachemann believed, he was looking at a legitimate major-league pitching prospect.

Lachemann also saw McGwire drive the ball out of the ballpark and came away impressed with his potential as a hitter as well.

What impressed Dedeaux, along with McGwire's physical ability, was his personality and mental approach to the game and life.

"I always have had a saying, 'Show me the parents and I'll tell you who you are,'" Dedeaux said. "He has great parents. He and his dad and I went to a ball game, and Mark impressed me with his personality and he was very intelligent. I told him he was a USC kind of athlete."

McGwire made up his mind to accept the scholarship offer from USC. It turned out to be the right choice, because two weeks later he received a letter in the mail from ASU saying that they had given out all of their scholarships but hoped he would consider attending ASU and coming out for the baseball team as a walk-on.

The morning after making up his mind to attend USC, McGwire woke up with pains in his stomach. He had eaten strawberry pie the night before with Lachemann and thought maybe that had made him sick.

"I tried to ignore the pain and went to school as usual, but I didn't make it through the day," McGwire said. "I ended up in the hospital with appendicitis."

The doctor also found that McGwire was suffering from mononucleosis. The combination of the appendectomy and mononucleosis forced McGwire to rest for several weeks before he could resume playing for the Claremont American Legion team. Because of his layoff, he would have needed more time to get himself back into pitching shape, so he spent the season playing first base and led his team into the state play-offs with a .415 average, 14 homers, and 53 RBIs.

Even though he had signed with USC, McGwire knew there was a chance he would not be going to college. He really wanted to play baseball, and if he was selected in the amateur draft and received a good-enough offer he was ready to tell Dedeaux and Lachemann thanks, but no thanks.

McGwire's name was called by the Montreal Expos in the eighth round of the 1981 draft, selected as both a pitcher and first baseman. Evaluating draft selections years later can be painful, and this was certainly a pick the Expos would like to have redone. Neither of their first two picks in the draft, Darren Dilks, a left-handed pitcher from Oklahoma State, and Jeff Carl, a shortstop from the University of Wisconsin at Oshkosh, ever made it to the majors.

Being picked in the eighth round, especially in an era when signing bonuses even for first-round picks rarely topped $100,000, made McGwire's decision to go to USC an easy one. The Expos' offer was $8,500, while McGwire computed the USC scholarship to be worth at least $50,000.

"I had never thought of going to college because I didn't think I'd enjoy it," McGwire said. "That was one of the best decisions I've ever made."

Instead of making long bus rides through small southern towns, McGwire packed his belongings and moved 50 miles from home to a dormitory on the USC campus. He wasn't entirely certain what to expect, but he was ready for the challenge.

3

USC

One of the first lessons McGwire learned at USC was that he was not going to please everybody all the time.

During his freshman year, a reporter from his hometown of Claremont came to USC and wrote such a scathing article about McGwire that his family tried to hide it from him. He learned about it only when a family member accidentally mentioned it during conversation at dinner one night.

McGwire said he wanted to see the story, but he did more than read it. He took it back to his college dorm room and pasted it up by his bed.

"It was the first thing I saw every morning and the last thing I saw at night," he said.

McGwire's work habits, having been taught by

his parents, always were exemplary, but it didn't hurt him to receive extra motivation to work even harder. The freshman year of college, especially when it includes living away from home for the first time, is a tough adjustment for anyone to make, and it's even harder to do it while trying to master a sport.

All McGwire wanted to do that season was fit in and play baseball. The school's sports information office asked everyone to fill out a form listing their accomplishments so it could be included in the media guide. McGwire left the question unanswered.

"They had to call my dad to find out," he said. "I just play because I want to have fun and improve."

USC had one of the best baseball traditions of any college in the country, having won the most national championships and having produced numerous players who went on to become major-league stars, including Fred Lynn, Steve Kemp, Dave Kingman, and Tom Seaver.

Reporters have often asked Dedeaux if he could have predicted that McGwire would one day join the ranks of those great players and lead the majors in homers and RBIs. His standard comment is that he could have predicted it just as well as he could have forecast that Seaver would win the Cy Young award three times.

It would have been tough for Dedeaux to make that prediction when McGwire was a freshman, because he saw almost all of his assignments that year as a pitcher. Dedeaux was reluctant to use freshmen often or in key situations, so it was more of a learning year off the field for McGwire.

Of his 29 appearances that year, 20 were as a pitcher. He was 4–4, with a very respectable 3.04 ERA. It didn't help that Lachemann, one of the big reasons McGwire had decided to come to USC, had stunned McGwire and the Trojans by announcing during the team's first meeting of the year that he was leaving to take a job in the Angels organization. McGwire has said that if Lachemann had not left USC, he might still be a pitcher.

"Larry Himes had called me and given me an offer to get back into pro ball as the Angels' minor-league pitching coordinator," Lachemann said. "It was an offer I didn't think I could turn down, so at the first players' meeting when we were getting everybody together for their winter instructions I announced that I was leaving. Mac looked me like I was nuts, saying, 'What's this, you recruited me and now you're leaving?' I've joked with him since that it was a good thing for him that I left or he might not have amounted to anything."

Offensively, McGwire's freshman year was a struggle. He hit an even .200 with three homers and 11 RBIs in 75 at-bats.

Still, there was something about his offensive promise that interested Ron Vaughn, an assistant coach for the Trojans who was heading to Alaska during the summer of 1982 to serve as an assistant coach for the Anchorage Glacier Pilots, a team in the Alaskan Summer League. He wanted to take McGwire with him—as a first baseman. The team had signed three first basemen, but none ever reached Alaska.

One was hurt, one signed a pro contract, and one took a different job for the summer. The Pilots had been offered Tim Wallach but, thinking they had enough first basemen, had sent him on to the team in Fairbanks.

Vaughn was impressed mainly with McGwire's work ethic and knew that if he set his mind to do something, he could most likely accomplish it.

"When he would take batting practice, he would analyze it and work on what he needed to do," Vaughn said. "He had a tough freshman year, because it's a big jump from high school to Division I, just like it's a big jump from college to the pros. He wasn't ready for it, but he was willing to work at it."

McGwire also wasn't ready for what greeted him upon his arrival in Alaska—a severe bout of homesickness. It was the first time in his life he had ever been that far away from home for an extended period of time, and it caused him many problems.

The Anchorage head coach was Jim Dietz, the head coach at San Diego State, and he and Vaughn spent a great deal of time with McGwire to try to help his mental well-being.

"He sat me down and we had a long talk," McGwire said of Dietz. "He told me that I was going to have to deal with being away from home a lot if I wanted to play pro ball. What he said made sense."

Dietz remembers one day in particular, when he and McGwire were talking in the outfield, down the left field line.

"He had big tears in his eyes and he was crying

and he really wanted to go home," Dietz said. "He was a lost young man at that point. I told him he wasn't going home."

Said Vaughn, "It was an adjustment because he didn't have his family and friends and school to fall back on. Once he thinks something through and looks at it from all sides he figures it out. That's what gets him through slumps or injuries or whatever. He's got a lot of mental toughness."

Vaughn's best memory of McGwire from that summer came in a game in which Don August, a future major-league pitcher, had a no-hitter going into the ninth inning in a 0–0 tie. McGwire came to bat and launched a long home run that not only cost August the no-hitter but also handed him the loss.

Dietz said he doesn't recall specific games from that season or any others, but he remembers the individuals and McGwire will always stand out in his memory.

"He had a lot of things cooking that summer, and I think everything that happened in Alaska was probably the foundation when he started to put everything together," Dietz said. "He had to sort out what he could do best. He had a comfort zone pitching, but if you watched batting practice, you could tell hitting was going to be his future."

Dietz instructed Vaughn to spend time with McGwire, providing as much support and counseling as possible, not just about baseball, but about growing up.

"The idea behind summer ball is for growth and

development," Dietz said. "The only way you can get better is by failure and working through that failure. You have to plant the seed and just watch it develop, and sometimes it takes a long time."

McGwire became a leader on the team that included future major leaguers Cory Snyder, Casey Candaele, and Mike Brumley. The team finished second in the National Baseball Congress tournament in Wichita, Kansas, losing in the finals to the team from Santa Maria, California.

McGwire led the Pilots with a .403 average, 53 RBIs, and 13 homers, perfecting the refinements in his swing and stance taught to him by Dietz and Vaughn. He ended up winning the league's batting title.

"The environment in Alaska really helped me," McGwire said when he returned to USC that fall. "I was away from home for the first time in my life with a group of people I didn't know. I didn't have the support of my family and girlfriend, and I went through a very bad period of homesickness. But instead of quitting and going home, which would have been the easy thing to do, I stuck it out. As a result, I gained confidence in myself, and I grew up."

Ever since their summer together, Dietz has followed McGwire's career, closer than McGwire ever realized until they met again before a game in San Diego in 1998. Dietz was wondering if McGwire would remember him, but when he walked into the Cardinals' locker room McGwire greeted him with a giant bear hug.

"He almost broke all of my vertebrae," Dietz said.

The summer in Alaska made McGwire stronger mentally and convinced him that he wanted to become a regular first baseman, getting the chance to play every day, instead of getting a chance to pitch once every four or five games.

When he made that pronouncement to Dedeaux before his sophomore year, the coach wasn't happy.

"Any time you have somebody who can swing the bat like he could even then, you know it's only a matter of time before they are playing someplace every day," Dedeaux said. "It was always my opinion, though, that you should keep your options open for as long as possible and not make a decision too soon."

Dedeaux had a lot of experience with moving players from one position to another when they came out of high school to USC.

"Most good athletes are either pitchers or shortstops in high school," Dedeaux said. "Fred Lynn came to us as a pitcher; so did Dave Kingman."

When some longtime USC followers first saw McGwire play, the player they instantly compared him to was Kingman, who had played at USC in 1969 and 1970, primarily because of their similar physical stature. As a pitcher in 1969, Kingman was 11–4, with a glittering 1.38 ERA. Playing exclusively in the field in 1970, Kingman hit .355 with nine homers, became a first-round draft pick of the Giants, and went on to a long major-league career—as an outfielder and first baseman.

One of the differences between Kingman and McGwire, Dedeaux recalled, was that Kingman was opposed to moving off the mound.

"Kingman wanted to pitch only," Dedeaux said. "And he had the ability to be a major-league pitcher. He had a loose arm and a real good curveball. He also was the kind of guy you just had to figure out a way to get in the lineup every day."

Years earlier, Dedeaux also had converted another pitcher to first baseman: Bill Seinsoth, a first-round pick of the Dodgers in 1969, who Dedeaux believes would have become the Dodgers' regular first baseman had he not been killed in an automobile accident.

"If he had lived you never would have heard of Steve Garvey," Dedeaux said.

McGwire was happy about playing more at first base, and to please Dedeaux he agreed to also pitch when necessary. He started seven games for the Trojans and made one relief appearance, producing a 3–1 record and lowering his ERA to 2.78.

"There was one scout who watched our games, Mickey McDermott, who had been a left-handed pitcher with the Red Sox, and he gave me hell about playing McGwire at first base," Dedeaux said. "He told me, 'He's the best pitching prospect I've seen.'"

McDermott and the other scouts also had to see that a pretty good power-hitting first base prospect was emerging as well. The summer of playing baseball and talking about the game every day with Vaughn, Dietz, and his teammates had made Mc-

Gwire a much more polished player than he had been as a freshman.

"He really got an education about baseball in Alaska, and also matured a lot as a person," Dedeaux said. "Both of those things helped him so much. Playing baseball is a tough profession, and he learned a lot about it that summer."

McGwire's buddy from grade school and high school, Randy Robertson, was one of McGwire's roommates in an apartment near the USC campus his sophomore year. That was when Robertson picked up on the fact that McGwire had become very organized and wanted everything kept neat and tidy.

"He thought me and our other roommate were slobs," Robertson said. "We didn't care about that stuff too much, and he was always getting upset when we made a mess and didn't clean it up. He cleaned up after us sometimes, but he eventually put a lock on his door to keep us out. I guess he figured at least then he had a room he could go to that would be clean."

That year was the first time Robertson noticed how involved McGwire had become with lifting weights.

"We would be there watching TV and he always had a weight in his hand, doing arm curls," Robertson said.

McGwire also experienced the first internal pressure of pursuing a home run record as a sophomore at USC, when a quick homer burst put him on pace to break the Trojans' single-season mark of 17. The record had been set by Kent Hadley in 1956 and equaled by future major leaguer Dave Hostetler in 1978.

Despite their glittering major-league careers, none of the "big" names who came through USC hit that many homers. The most Lynn hit in a season was 14; Steve Kemp's best was 13; Kingman's best was the nine he hit in 1970.

"I didn't hit that many at the beginning of the season, but then all of a sudden I went on a tear, hitting two a series, three a series, and even four a series," McGwire said. "There's a big board in our clubhouse with all of the records, and one day I looked up and saw 17 home runs for one season.

"That's not really much today if you look at all the people hitting 20 and even 30 home runs. I said to myself, 'That's not that much and I hope I can break it.' "

After tying the record, McGwire fell into a slump and went seven games without a homer before finally connecting for the record breaker in the second game of a doubleheader at California.

"It's not unusual for me to go without a home run in that span of games," McGwire said at the time. "But since I had been on a home run tear, everyone was saying, 'What's wrong and what are you doing?'

"I started pressing myself because I wanted it really bad, and doing that I got into a real bad slump during the Arizona series. I went 1-for-12.

"I didn't feel comfortable at the plate. I had it on my mind all the time. I was getting great pitches to hit; I just wasn't hitting them. When we played Long Beach State, I just concentrated on hitting the ball the other way and getting relaxed and I started hitting the ball well."

When he saw the record-breaking homer finally disappear over the left center field wall, McGwire was ready to celebrate.

"It was a line drive with good-enough height to get out," he told reporters covering that game. "I hit it well and I knew it was going. I knew I had it and I could get down to playing baseball again and not have to worry about the record anymore.

"When I hit it, I felt it would be nice to have the ball. But it landed in a bunch of cement slabs and wood and rubble just beyond the fence. [USC catcher] Jack Del Rio's cousin went out there and dug it out for me."

McGwire added another homer before the season ended, giving him 19. He finished the year with a .319 average and 59 RBIs in 53 games, at the time the sixth-highest single-season RBI total in USC history.

His performance was good enough to earn him a spot on a USA team that was going to spend the summer playing a tough schedule aganst international competition. Sponsored by the U.S. Baseball Federation as a pre-Olympic team, the U.S. squad played Japan and Korea in games around the United States and also competed in Tokyo and China, at the International Cup Games in Belgium, and at the Pan-American Games in Venezuela.

Despite losing 15 pounds during his stay in Venezuela when he lost his appetite, McGwire helped lead the U.S. squad to a third-place finish at the Pan-American Games behind Cuba and Nicaragua. McGwire hit .454 (15-of-33) with six homers, two doubles, and two triples.

McGwire's U.S. squad also finished second to Cuba in the International Cup Games in Belgium, and McGwire said while it was great to play against top international teams, he actually learned more and got more personal attention and instruction the previous summer when he was playing in Alaska.

"People say to me how exciting it must be to see all these different countries, but quite honestly, all we did was play the games and go back to the hotel," McGwire said at the end of that summer. "There was a lot of pressure on our coaches to win in these international games."

The most memorable games were against Cuba, and even though the U.S. was routed 8–1 by the Cubans in the Gold Medal game of the Pan-American Games, McGwire came away impressed with the talent from the small country.

"I didn't do very well against them," he said. "It was like playing a professional team. Their pitching was outstanding. They did everything well. When Barbaro Garbey [a Tiger rookie in 1984] was on the Cuban team in 1979, he was on the bench. That tells you something about their talent."

Returning to USC for his junior year, McGwire found another home run record to shoot for—the career mark of 32, set by Pat Harrison between 1966 and 1968. With 22 homers going into the season, the mark seemed to be an easy target.

McGwire's performance in his sophomore year, and the summer following, also had erased any doubt about his future after USC. He was now established as a preseason All-America selection and an almost definite first-round pick in the amateur draft following the season. The only question was whether his stock would go up or down based on his efforts during the year.

McGwire had no hesitation in admitting that he was at USC for baseball first and school second. A 2.8 GPA student in high school, McGwire had maintained good-enough grades in college, with a C average, to remain eligible for baseball. Since he had to declare a major before his junior year, he picked public administration. If for some reason his baseball career had not been so successful, McGwire has said many times, he probably would have become a police officer.

Those concerns were not on his mind at the time, however, and Vaughn, even though he had moved on from USC to other schools, was watching his prize pupil with a great deal of pride. They had continued their friendship and baseball education through private instructions, and McGwire still considers Vaughn, now scouting for Oakland, one of the best instructors and coaches he has ever had.

"He still had a long swing, and we worked on getting it shorter," Vaughn said. "He was always able to take instructions and ideas and work on them until he got them down. He was basically the same guy then that he is now. He never says a lot, but he just works at what he's doing."

McGwire was trying to put the final touches on a great college career, and that's exactly what he did. Not only did he smash USC's career home run record; he matched it in a single season, hitting 32 homers in 67 games. His total also broke the Pac-10 Conference record for most homers in a season, which had been 29, set by UCLA's Jim Auten in 1979, and also broke the conference career record as well. His pitching career was over.

He hit long home runs then, as well. One shot against Arizona State cleared the 425-foot fence in center field at Dedeaux Field and the parking structure behind the fence. At Arizona, he hit one homer over a huge scoreboard in left field and in the same game hit a homer to right that went so far nobody saw it land.

During batting practice once, McGwire's line drive carried over the left field wall and collided with the windshield of a BMW. Robertson said, "Someone wrote 'ouch' on the window."

McGwire still holds both the single-season and career home run records at USC. A year after his career ended, the fences at Dedeaux Field were moved back.

"The joke was that my dad paid to have them moved back so that no one would break my record," McGwire kiddingly said several years later.

Despite his home run total, he heard some criticism from scouts and doubt about his professional ability—comments such as the only thing he could do was hit home runs. Since he was using an aluminum bat and would have to switch to wood in the pros, there were doubters who didn't think he would be able to continue to hit as many homers and hit them as far as he was doing in college.

"I've heard from a few scouts that all I could do is hit the long ball," McGwire said. "I just hope I can show them that I can do other things. I'd like to be known as a guy who can hit the long ball, hit for a pretty good average, and be good defensively."

McGwire spent a lot of time that season working on his defense at first base, saying he got almost as excited making a good diving stop as he did hitting a home run.

He also spent a year learning how to adjust to different styles of pitching, since his big sophomore season had made him a target and focus point for opposing pitchers. Only rarely did a pitcher try to throw a fastball by him anymore; instead, they concentrated on throwing him off-speed pitches and curveballs.

McGwire proved he could hit those pitches as well, and for average as well as homers. He led the Trojans in virtually every offensive category, hitting .387 and driving in 80 runs to go along with his 32 homers. He also had 20 doubles and showed his patience at the plate by walking 50 times and striking out only 33 times in 248 at bats.

Robertson remembers one game from that season when he was pitching against Loyola of Marymount and accidentally hit a batter. A brawl ensued, but Robertson was not involved in the fight. McGwire was.

"I got kicked out of the game for fighting," Robertson said. "I started to protest, but Coach Dedeaux came over to me and said, 'Randy, go ahead and leave. We've got lots of pitchers, but we've only got one Mark McGwire.' "

McGwire gave a lot of credit for his success to Dedeaux, who he said taught him how to improve mentally as well as physically working on developing his skills.

Dedeaux was quick to return the compliment. "He was a gentleman," Dedeaux said.

At least two scouting directors for major-league clubs were convinced that McGwire was the best player available in the draft. One of those was Joe McIlvaine, the scouting director and future general manager of the Mets, the team with the number-one overall pick. The other was Dick Wiencek of the Oakland A's, who had a little bit of an edge because of a home-field advantage. He lived in McGwire's hometown of Claremont, five blocks away from McGwire's home.

Despite knowing McGwire and his family so well and having watched him develop over the years, Wiencek did not spend much time watching McGwire play that season because he didn't think there was any way McGwire would be available when it came time for the A's to make their first-round pick, the 10th spot in the draft.

Baseball America, the national publication that does the best job in the country of predicting the draft and surveying scouts for their opinions on the ranking of players, had McGwire ranked as the 10th best overall prospect in the draft. The five position players ranked above him were Shawn Abner, a high school outfielder from Pennsylvania; Cory Snyder, a shortstop (at the time) from Brigham Young; Shane Mack, an outfielder from UCLA; Oddibe McDowell, an outfielder from Arizona State; and Jay Bell, a high school shortstop from Florida.

In its predraft evaluation, *Baseball America*'s capsule on McGwire said in part: "most scouting directors agree that he is the leading power-hitting prospect available in the draft, but some insist his big home run bat won't land him in the upper half of the first round. 'There are just too many things he doesn't do well enough to rate being considered a premium pick,' said one scouting director. Another says he's becoming a competent first baseman, but 'he would go higher in the draft if he showed he could play third base or another position.' For all his power, some also say he can't handle the inside pitch."

McIlvaine had none of those worries. As scouting director, he personally didn't get to see McGwire play as often as the area scouts, but he did watch him in a game on May 7, approximately a month before the draft, and turned in a report that indicated the following:

With a top grade of 8, McIlvaine gave McGwire a 7 for hitting ability and 8s for power and power frequency. McIlvaine reported that McGwire had above-average arm strength and was an average fielder with above-average instincts.

McIlvaine's summary said: "A horse of a man. He has really trimmed down and firmed up in three years. A Tim Wallach type of player."

Under "Strengths," McIlvaine said: "Capable of leading major leagues in home runs and RBIs in future. Good short stroke with very few strikeouts for home run hitter. Fielding at first base has greatly improved. Strong arm, good hands, good makeup, a winner."

Under "Weaknesses," the only thing McIlvaine mentioned was lack of good running speed.

"For our needs a position shift from first base to third base would be a most tempting proposition," McIlvaine's report concluded. "Could hit in middle of lineup and give us additional RBI man we need. Will get to the major leagues very quickly. Excellent prospect."

Since McIlvaine was in charge of the Mets' draft, he was convinced McGwire was going to be the choice. He was the top-rated player on their board following the predraft staff meetings.

The night before the draft, McIlvaine placed a telephone call to McGwire's father in California. The call lasted for 45 minutes, and no dollar figure was ever mentioned. According to McIlvaine, the only question he kept asking was, "If we take your son with the number-one pick in the draft tomorrow, would be consider signing with the Mets?"

"He wouldn't give us an answer," McIlvaine said. "He said they needed more time, that he couldn't give us an answer. I was upset, but I was trying not to project that to the father. We kept saying, 'We're going to make your son the number-one choice in the country.' He kept waxing and asking for more time."

McIlvaine said when he has encountered resistance from parents of other potential draft picks he often believes an agent has entered the picture. He didn't believe that was the situation in this case and thinks the only two factors working against the Mets were beyond his control—the team had not been very good in recent years, and he got the feeling that the elder McGwire wanted his son to go to a team on the West Coast.

"That's the thing about the draft," McIlvaine said. "You can do all the scouting you want and get everybody in order, but if you can't sign the player you waste the pick, and you don't want to waste the number-one overall pick."

Frustrated after speaking to John McGwire, McIlvaine called the parents of Shawn Abner, the high school player from Mechanicsburg, Pennsylvania, and the player ranked number two on the Mets' draft board. McIlvaine asked Abner the same question about signing with the Mets and was met with a resounding yes.

When the draft began the next morning, the Mets chose Abner.

"We liked him a lot, too," McIlvaine said. "He was a five-tool high school player."

Unfortunately for the Mets, Abner never developed as a major leaguer, the risk every scouting director takes when he makes a selection.

The McGwire side's recollections of the 24 hours preceding the draft differ from McIlvaine's memory. Bob Cohen, an attorney who has represented McGwire since the draft, told *Baseball America* that the Mets "put pressure on him that day to sign. They wanted him to do a contract that day, and he said, 'I'm not going to do a contract that day.'"

Whatever the fallout was with the Mets, Wiencek was watching the draft unfold from a conference room in Oakland and he could barely sit still in his chair.

Seattle had the second pick and took a college pitcher, Billy Swift. Another pitcher, Drew Hall, went third, to the Cubs, followed by Snyder, who was the fourth pick by the Indians. Choosing fifth, the Reds took college pitcher Pat Pacillo, and the Angels, next in line, went for a high school catcher, Erik Pappas.

Where was McGwire? Why wasn't anybody taking him, Oakland GM Sandy Alderson wanted to know. "What don't we know about this guy?" Alderson recalled saying. "What is it we don't know that everybody else knows?"

The Cardinals chose college pitcher Mike Dunne with the seventh pick, and the Twins followed with Bell. There was just one team remaining now before the A's turn, the Giants. When San Francisco selected Alan Cockrell, a college outfielder, Wiencek did come flying out of his chair.

"We were tickled that we got him," Wiencek said. "Our owners didn't want me to take a first baseman, so I told them we would move him to third. I just had a feeling about him. Other guys have taken credit for it over the years, but I put my job on the line to take him. I know what happened. I was there."

Alderson believes McGwire fell from first to 10th because a lot of teams likely were scared when he would not make a commitment to sign with the Mets. Also, as teams did their predraft evaluations in many cases they settled in on a particular player and were ready to take him no matter what happened with other teams and other players.

That was fine with the A's, and even they didn't realize just how good a player they were getting.

Even after McGwire signed, for a bonus of $125,000, he had one more stop to make before beginning his pro career—the Olympic Games.

4

GOING FOR THE GOLD

The two previous summers had been hectic, playing in Alaska in 1982 and touring the world on a select U.S. team in 1983, but McGwire would learn a new definition of the word as he and the rest of the U.S. squad prepared for the 1984 Olympics in Los Angeles.

Baseball was a demonstration sport at these Olympics, and the U.S. definitely wanted to do well, considering it was America's game and the Olympics were being conducted at Dodger Stadium.

The coaches and administrators in charge of the U.S. team, which included Dedeaux, thought the best way to prepare the team was with an extensive exhibition schedule that featured games all across the country.

In hindsight, the schedule that seemed only a bit ambitious looks rather intense, and it likely contributed to the U.S. team being tired and overworked when the actual Olympic competition began.

The tryouts for the team were held in Louisville, and even though McGwire had played for Dedeaux and was considered an automatic selection, he still had to go through the workouts and practice games with the rest of the candidates. There, he renewed his relationship with John Scolinos, the coach who taught McGwire in one of his summer clinics when he was a youngster.

Even though Scolinos was working with the pitchers at the Olympic trials, he, like everyone else, stopped what he was doing and watched when McGwire stepped up to take batting practice.

"Louisville had a big ballpark, like maybe 400 feet to the left field wall," Scolinos said. "Beyond that is a bridge that spans a four-lane highway. One afternoon I saw McGwire hit a ball that not only left the park but also cleared the bridge on the other side. I estimated at the time that the ball went 500 feet. Looking back, I think I might have been too conservative."

Dedeaux was used to seeing McGwire's long homers, as was Art Mazmanian, the junior college coach who had recommended McGwire to USC. Mazmanian also was traveling with the Olympic team as an assistant coach.

Maybe because Dedeaux and the other coaches knew McGwire better than they knew some of the other players, they expected him to become one of the leaders of the team and to set his typical example of working hard, hoping for it to rub off.

"I think the entire Olympic experience helped him tremendously because he had an opportunity to be a leader on the club and it was a great experience playing under pressure conditions," Dedeaux said.

What McGwire remembers most about the pre-Olympic tour, other than his teammates, was the brutal travel schedule and how tired he and the other players were all of the time. In a five-week span, the team played 35 games in 33 cities. In one stretch, they played 19 games in 19 days in 19 different cities. McGwire was in New York for the first time in his life and recalls seeing nothing but the inside of his hotel room and Shea Stadium.

The team would play a game in one city, get to bed late in a hotel, wake up early the next morning, fly or bus to the next city, check into the hotel, play the game, and then repeat the cycle again the following day. Wherever he went, McGwire usually put on a show, either during the game or in batting practice.

Mazmanian remembered one game in Memphis when McGwire used a wooden bat that he borrowed from Oddibe McDowell in a game. He hit three shots that all went against the wall.

"If he had been using a metal bat he would have had three homers for sure," Mazmanian said.

During one game at Fenway Park in Boston, McGwire hit a particularly long home run and it so happened that future Hall of Famer Reggie Jackson was sitting on the U.S. bench, next to Dedeaux, at that moment.

"Mark hit a ball that went off the back wall behind the center field bleachers," Dedeaux said. "Reggie said he had never seen a ball hit that far. I know Mark was using an aluminum bat, but it still was unbelievable. He put on some exhibitions that you couldn't believe."

The homer, which Jackson called "a [bleeping] rocket," was estimated at 450 feet. Jackson, playing for the Angels at the time, made it a point to go up and talk to McGwire. Jackson told him, "Son, when you hit a ball like that, you've got to watch it."

McGwire was polite but disagreed. "No," he said. "That's not my style."

It also wasn't McGwire's style to pay too much attention to baseball history. The U.S. team's tour included a stop at the Baseball Hall of Fame in Cooperstown, New York, the first time McGwire had ever been to the shrine of his sport. While many team members toured the museum, McGwire and some of his buddies went to a pizza parlor.

The toughest thing about playing on the team, said McGwire and others, was the competition. The talent level was so great that the coaches struggled to decide who was going to play and who was going to be a reserve. With everybody on the team used to being the star on his own club, there definitely were some ego problems.

The other first baseman on the team with McGwire was Will Clark, the future star with the Giants and Rangers. Clark and McGwire became friendly rivals, though they both received spots in the lineup when Clark was the designated hitter and McGwire played first.

"Nobody ever took a swing at anybody, at least not that I know of," McGwire said. "But there was a lot of ragging going on, and some of it was kidding on the square."

The team featured future major leaguers B. J. Surhoff, Barry Larkin, Shane Mack, Oddibe McDowell, Cory Snyder, Billy Swift, Bobby Witt, Scott Bankhead, Chris Gwynn, and others. Of the 20 players who survived the final cut before the Games, 18 were first-round picks in the amateur draft and 16 later played in the majors.

"Quite probably, we made up the best amateur team in the history of America," McGwire said.

McGwire finished the 37-game pre-Olympic tour with a .359 average, six homers, and 26 RBIs. Clark was the team's best player heading into Los Angeles, having hit .397 with 16 homers and 43 RBIs.

Before the Olympics, Dedeaux asked McGwire about carrying the flag for the U.S. team before the opening baseball ceremonies at Dodger Stadium. McGwire said no thanks, that he wanted to march in with the rest of his teammates, so Dedeaux had pitcher Billy Swift carry the flag.

Still, just being a part of all the festivities of the entire Olympics, at the Los Angeles Coliseum and at Dodger Stadium, was special for McGwire.

"Walking into the opening ceremonies, in front

of the 100,000 fans and a billion people watching on TV, I don't think there's another feeling like that," McGwire said.

Despite all of the hype and achievements of the individual players, the U.S. failed to win the Gold Medal. The team genuinely considered the best amateur team in the world, Cuba, wasn't even at the games, instead participating in the Soviet boycott.

The U.S. won its preliminary games, topping a strong team from Taipei 2–1 in the opener before blasting Italy 16–1 and routing the Dominican Republic 12–0. In the medal round, the U.S. defeated South Korea 5–2 behind a two-run homer by McDowell and a two-run double by Snyder to reach the Gold Medal game, against Japan.

McGwire had not contributed much in those victories, collecting only three singles. He delivered a key hit against Japan that should have produced a run, but Chris Gwynn tripped running the bases and was thrown out, which took the U.S. out of a potential big inning.

Japan won the game, 6–3, to capture the Gold Medal, leaving McGwire and the rest of the U.S. squad disappointed. During the tour before the Olympics, the U.S. had defeated the Japanese team in six of their seven meetings.

Of all the players on the U.S. team, one who made a lasting impression on McGwire was McDowell, his Pac-10 rival from Arizona State who shared the league's MVP award with him that season.

"I really looked up to Oddibe because of the way

he went about practice—hitting, running hard, shagging flies every day no matter how tired we got," McGwire said. "I really respected his professionalism."

There has been talk in more recent Olympics of using professional baseball players to represent the U.S., as has been the case in other sports such as basketball and hockey, but McGwire doesn't think that will ever happen. For one thing, the timing of the Games is wrong, coming usually at the end of August or beginning of September, right in the middle of the pennant battles. For another, McGwire thinks it is a great opportunity for college players and should remain their show.

"I don't believe in professionals being in the Olympics," McGwire said. "There are great amateur athletes in the colleges. They should go for the gold."

With the Olympics over for him, it was time for McGwire to go somewhere himself. He packed his car and headed north to Modesto, California, ready to begin his life as a professional baseball player.

5

THE MINORS

By the time he reached Modesto, McGwire realized how tired he was. He had played a full year of baseball, starting with his college season at USC, going through the U.S. Olympic tour and then the intensity of the Games themselves. Now he was being asked to shift gears and start the learning process all over again. He also was suffering from a pulled hamstring muscle that limited his availability.

"He was flat worn out," recalled Grady Fuson, a coach at Modesto in 1984 and now Oakland's scouting director. "You could tell how tired he was. He was still trying to get his feet on the ground."

As a result, the A's didn't expect much from McGwire in his pro debut except to meet some of the people he would be working with, including some of his new teammates, and perhaps get rid of some of the tension that might accompany becoming a professional.

Because of his notoriety, however, some observers expected McGwire to be an instant success and start launching homer after homer. When it didn't happen immediately, they said he was a bust.

Dick Wiencek took exception to that, in large part because he had such a personal stake in whether the selection of McGwire turned out to be a hit or a miss.

One reason for McGwire's slow start was that turning professional meant switching from an aluminum to a wooden bat, an adjustment many young hitters struggle to make.

"It took him a while," Wiencek said. "When he didn't hit well right away I got second-guessed, but I told everybody to give it a little more time. 'If he doesn't hit good next year,' I said, 'then I will tell you I made a mistake.'"

McGwire's first professional manager was George Mitterwald, the former major-league catcher. He was prepared to give McGwire some extra time to get comfortable as a pro, rather than being too judgmental.

"He had to make some adjustments," Mitterwald said. "People don't realize it, but it takes time. I don't care who the player is."

McGwire finished the year in Modesto by playing in 16 games. He struck out 21 times in 55 at-bats but did hit his first professional homer and finished with a .200 average. He also joined in on his first league championship as Modesto, despite finishing second in the northern division during the regular season, beat Redwood and Bakersfield in the play-offs to win the title.

After allowing him some time at home to rest, the A's asked McGwire to report to their Instructional League team in Arizona, where they wanted to find out if he could make the move across the infield and become a third baseman.

When Wiencek had told his bosses that he would convert McGwire to third if they allowed him to draft McGwire, he didn't know what might happen. The more the people in the organization discussed the idea, however, the more sense it made.

The A's already had a young power-hitting first baseman in the organization, Rob Nelson, whom they had selected in the first round of the 1983 draft. Playing at Class A Madison in the Midwest League in 1984, Nelson had hit 19 homers and driven in 84 runs.

Physically, Nelson was almost identical with Mc-Gwire—he was 6-foot-4, an inch shorter than Mc-Gwire, and weighed 215 pounds, only a few pounds less than McGwire. The big difference was that Nelson batted and threw left-handed, which meant he could not switch positions unless he moved to the outfield.

"Rob was a half step ahead of McGwire because he had been drafted the year before," Grady Fuson said. "He was a corner guy with a lot of power, and we had high hopes for him."

The organization saw Nelson and a couple of other good young prospects, outfielder Jose Canseco and catcher Terry Steinbach, advancing through the farm system. If McGwire could make the switch to third base it would allow each of them a place to play and prosper.

"Mark had very good feet, good hands, and the arm strength to do it," Fuson said. "Those are the things you look for in a corner guy. He didn't have a lot of feel for throwing across the field, but I'm sure he could have learned that over the years."

McGwire was willing to try anything, and he went to the Instructional League and worked hard at learning the new position.

Fred Stanley, who now works for the Brewers, was the A's director of instruction at the time and he took McGwire under his wing and began to work with him on a daily basis.

"I think what Fred was trying to do was toughen Mark up," said Keith Lieppman, at the time a minor-league manager for the A's and now the team's director of player development. "When he hit ground balls to Mark, he tried to hit them hard enough that it would hit Mark on either the wrist or the shin. Every time he did it, he would let out this high-pitched whistle that you could hear all across the field.

"It drove Mark crazy. They played that game every day in Instructional League and during spring training. Every time he hit him, Stanley would laugh and make that noise. To this day Mark laughs about it. He said then that when he retired as a player he wanted me to leave a job open for him so he could come back and teach guys how to become great fielders."

Stanley recalls the time he spent with McGwire as quite enjoyable, despite the fact, he says, that McGwire told him, "If I ever get my hands on you, I'm going to kill you."

McGwire wasn't the only Stanley pupil who made that good-natured claim after a day of getting pounded on the shin, wrist, and various other body parts.

"I really wanted to get them to concentrate," Stanley said about all of the players he worked with, including McGwire. "I smoked it at them. If I caught some skin, I made a whistle like getting hit by a car. I played games with them and tried to keep it fun. It's hard to go out there in the hot sun every day and get beat up by some guy with a fungo bat."

Even then Stanley was impressed by McGwire's work habits and predicted he would become a successful major leaguer.

"He was very determined," Stanley said. "He came early and he stayed late. He was an awfully big guy to try to learn to play third base, but he worked at it. Whatever he has achieved he has earned."

There even was a patch of rocky ground at the A's complex, and McGwire took countless ground balls there, trying to practice some of the bad hops and unusual bounces he was certain to get playing on uneven minor-league fields for the next couple of years.

"He went through a lot of physical abuse trying to learn to play the position," said Lieppman, who managed McGwire during his short stay at Triple A Tacoma, Washington, in 1986. "He also received a lot of mental abuse. There was a fan in Tacoma who sat along the third base line and always let him have it.

"For a lot of people it really would have been a negative experience, but I think it made him tough and is part of the reason why he's the player he is now."

One night during the 1984 Instructional League, the A's staff arranged to have a party at a Mexican restaurant in Scottsdale. Ted Polakowski, at the time a minor-league trainer and now the director of Arizona baseball operations, was in charge of the arrangements, but he couldn't leave until everyone else had left the practice facility.

McGwire and Nelson, both of whom had been at the facility since 7:00 A.M., were still taking batting practice well after dark, working with Karl Kuehl, the A's director of player development.

"I was standing at the door, and they were maybe 150 yards away from me, and I couldn't see them," Polakowski said. "That's how dark it was. But I could hear them. All I heard was the crack of the bat meeting the ball."

Even after the three came in from batting practice, McGwire and Nelson still spent time lifting weights before finally calling it a day and letting Polakowski leave for his party.

Kuehl said the difference between McGwire and

other minor-league players coming up through the organization was that McGwire possessed so much raw natural ability that he had never had to work to be one of the best players on his team. Now that he was a professional, however, his already-good work habits needed to improve even more—and they did.

"Everything had always come so easy for him," Kuehl said. "What he had to do was learn to work. I have to give him a lot of credit for that."

The A's sent McGwire back to Modesto for the 1985 season, hoping he could regain his power stroke while also playing adequately at third base. The results were mixed. He did return to form offensively, hitting 24 homers and driving in 106 runs. Both totals were good enough to tie for the league lead. Defensively, however, McGwire struggled, committing 33 errors. The team finished the year in second place again but this time lost in the first round of the playoffs.

"The problems he had offensively came on breaking stuff and when he was trying to pull everything, even the pitches away," said Dick Bogard, an A's scout who saw McGwire play a lot that season. "All of a sudden it was like a light went on and the pitches he was having trouble with he started smoking. From that point on he took off."

For four months Mitterwald tried to convince McGwire to move toward the pitcher and closer to the plate. He would make the adjustment in batting practice, but then when the game started he would fall back into his comfort zone of almost standing out of the box.

"He couldn't reach the breaking ball away, and a lot of pitchers were eating him up," Mitterwald said. "I knew if he moved closer to the plate pitchers were going to try to bust him inside, and that was the pitch he was going to have to learn how to hit.

"One night Bob Watson was at the game. He was a roving hitting instructor for the A's, and his career average was about .300. Mark was taking batting practice, from his normal stance, and Watson said to him, 'Mark, did you ever think about moving up closer to the plate?' He said, 'You know what? That's a good idea.'

"He did it that night during the game and hit two homers and he's done it ever since."

Opposing pitchers and managers quickly learned about McGwire and his ability.

"He had awesome power even then," said Wendell Kim, who managed the Giants' farm team at Fresno in 1984 and 1985 and now is the third base coach for the Red Sox. "He still had a lot of holes in his swing, and he loved the fastball middle in and up over the plate. At times he had trouble with good breaking pitches and split-fingered fastballs, but the pitchers who didn't throw very hard had to rely on good location.

"The fences in the league weren't very far, so when Mark hit them it looked like it was really going a long way."

When he wasn't playing, McGwire usually was watching a baseball game. Modesto was only about an hour's drive from the Oakland Coliseum, and frequently during the season when both teams were at home A's officials would look into the stands during day games and spot McGwire, calmly watching batting practice and the game.

"I couldn't think of anything I'd rather be doing," was McGwire's explanation.

He hadn't called anyone for tickets or arranged for a special parking place but had bought a ticket and walked from the parking lot just like every other fan.

What McGwire saw was a major-league team in transition. The players were getting younger, and he no doubt pictured himself down on the field, playing, within a very short period of time.

The managers in the California League were quick to recognize McGwire's talent and that he was a player on the rise to the majors. In *Baseball America*'s annual survey of the league's managers at the end of the season trying to identify the best major-league prospects, McGwire was ranked fourth.

Ranked ahead of him were three pitching prospects from Milwaukee, all of whom had played at Stockton that year—Jeff Parrett, Dan Murphy, and Alex Madrid.

"One unidentified manager said he [McGwire] was the league's best prospect," *Baseball America* said. "Another said that, for all the improvement he showed this season, he might eventually have to return to first base, or even pitching—his original position at USC.

"At any rate, McGwire had major adjustments to

overcome—hitting with wooden bats, shifting from first to third base—and managers took note, voting him the league's most improved player. They also said he was the player with the best power in the league, although one manager said he didn't have a feel for the ball as a hitter."

Other players ranked in the league's top 10 prospects included McGwire's former Olympic teammate Will Clark, Visalia (Minnesota) shortstop Jay Bell, and Giants third base prospect Charlie Hayes.

Another player, ranked sixth, was Eric Hardgrave, a first baseman from Reno, a San Diego farm team, who tied McGwire for the league lead with 24 homers. Hardgrave hit his before July, when he was moved out of the league. He never made it to the majors.

The player McGwire tied for the RBI title was Gene Larkin, a first baseman at Visalia who did make it to the majors with the Twins.

One player who quickly took a liking to McGwire at Modesto was shortstop Walt Weiss, who joined the team for the final month of the season after being promoted from rookie ball. His first night in town, he was in the starting lineup, hitting leadoff and playing shortstop, when McGwire came up to him in the dugout a few minutes before the game was going to begin.

"Mark came up to me and said when they announce the lineup and call out your name, we run onto the field and take our positions, one by one," said Weiss, a future teammate for years in Oakland

and now the shortstop of the Braves. "I was the first name called, and I ran out to shortstop. It was quickly obvious that that wasn't the case, because nobody else ran out. The game didn't start for 10 more minutes. I looked in the dugout and Mark was laughing his head off. I ran back off the field. I still might have to get back to him for that someday."

Mitterwald was quite pleased with the progress McGwire had made and with the effort he had put in to try to turn himself into a third baseman.

"We would spend about 20 or 30 minutes a day before the game working on fielding bunts and slow rollers," Mitterwald said. "For somebody his size to run in and throw the ball underhanded is real hard. He was doing pretty good.

"He was playing third one day and somebody hit a shot right at him, a one-hopper. He caught it and threw the guy out. As he came into the dugout, this big, tough guy said, 'Man, that was a toughie-woughie.' From that day on I used to tease him about it."

Mitterwald saw McGwire again in 1988, when Mitterwald was coaching for the Yankees and the A's came into New York.

"I don't know if he knew I was one of the coaches or not, but the A's were taking batting practice and I snuck up behind him and tapped him on the back and said, 'You had any toughie-woughies lately?' That broke him up."

At Modesto, McGwire again crossed paths with his childhood friend Randy Robertson, who was pitching for Reno, San Diego's farm team in the Cal League. Robertson doesn't remember facing Mc-Gwire that season but does remember one game when McGwire lost his temper.

"He got kicked out in the first inning for arguing the balls and strikes calls," Robertson said.

In *Baseball America*'s annual survey of prospects in each organization that winter, McGwire was ranked as the sixth-best prospect in the Oakland farm system, trailing Jose Canseco, Eric Plunk, Brian Dorsett, Rob Nelson, and Darrell Akerfelds. He was ahead of Tim Belcher, Luis Polonia, Stan Javier, and Weiss, an indication of how talent-loaded was the A's organization in the mid-1980s.

Canseco had been named *Baseball America*'s Minor League Player of the Year for 1985 and was ready to join the A's, where he didn't have to wait long before he was joined by McGwire.

McGwire spent the winter between the 1985 and 1986 seasons working on his own to improve his batting stroke, and some of those sessions were held at Mount San Antonio Junior College with his old mentor from USC and Alaska, Ron Vaughn.

Vaughn remembers one day very clearly.

"I always pitched with a screen in front of me, but one day I peeked out a little too far and he hit a liner right back at me that hit me and knocked me down," Vaughn said. "I couldn't breathe, and he didn't know what to do.

"He picked me up and carried me out of there. The ball had hit me right underneath my rib and just knocked the wind out of me. I had good seams for a while, but otherwise was OK. As soon as I could talk I told him, 'I think you've got it down now.' "

McGwire was promoted to Double A Huntsville, Alabama, for the beginning of the 1986 season, a reward for his success and hard work and proof that the A's were including him in their future plans.

One area that really impressed A's officials was the way McGwire had toned down his aggressiveness in criticizing umpires when a call went against him.

McGwire said he knew he had a tendency to get upset at times but just decided one night that he didn't want to act that way anymore. The moment came as he sat on the bench and watched another upset player launch into a major tirade.

"I saw another player act ridiculous and I looked at myself in the mirror and said, 'I look like that?' " McGwire said. "From that day on I stopped it. I didn't know I looked that stupid when I was doing that."

Lieppman still talks a lot about McGwire to young players in the A's organization, and he also shows them a video of McGwire in action—not hitting homers, but reacting when a call or an at-bat doesn't go his way.

"He really learned to control his temper," Lieppman said. "He used to be outrageous when he got frustrated. Now even when he strikes out he's very calm. We show the video to our kids so they can learn how they are supposed to act. He's a model citizen."

The jump to Double A is generally considered the toughest in the minors, with most scouts and person-

nel directors believing that it is the real proving
ground for prospects. Most believe that if a player is
successful at Double A, there's no reason to believe
he can't be successful in the majors.

McGwire had no trouble making the jump. The
full year of playing with a wooden bat in 1985 and
his work in the Instructional League and in spring
training left him prepared and ready for the challenge. He lasted less than half the season in the
Southern League, hitting .305 with 10 homers and 53
RBIs in 55 games before he got the word on June 6
that he was moving up to Tacoma in the Triple A Pa-
cific Coast League, one stop away from the majors.

"He's gotten bigger and stronger, but he's always
had power," Lieppman said. "I remember he joined
us at Phoenix, and that park's center field fence was
about 420 feet away. In his first game he hit a ball
over the big green monster there. That was kind of
his initiation to Triple A."

Lieppman was excited to finally have McGwire
on his team and add him to the mix of players he
thought were on the verge of making the A's a successful major-league club—Nelson, Javier, and Polonia, along with the likes of Canseco, who was
already in Oakland, and Steinbach and Weiss, who
were still on the way.

From the time he had first watched McGwire in
the Instructional League, Lieppman noticed a lot of
improvement in a short time.

"He learned to pace himself," Lieppman said.
"Everything he did he worked hard at and he did it

with a purpose. If he was hitting off a tee in batting practice, he would take his time, step out and re-gather himself. When he was working he knew exactly what he was trying to do. He just had a tremendous work ethic and would hit bucket after bucket of balls. He realized that was going to pay off for him."

When Lieppman had first seen McGwire, he was concerned about his swing and that it might be too long to be successful against major-league pitching. At Tacoma, he saw that the problem had been corrected.

"He truly had evolved," Lieppman said. "Little by little he made adjustments to shorten his swing down. Now it's very quick and short. He was able to make the adjustments that Nelson wasn't able to make."

Nelson already was playing first at Tacoma when McGwire joined the team and was in the midst of a successful season. Nelson's homer total declined from 32 (at Double A Huntsville in 1995) to 20, but he was making better contact and raised his average from .232 to .276.

"The idea was that with Nelson at first and Mc-Gwire at third we would have two power-hitting guys in the lineup to go with our other good young play-ers," Lieppman said. "When you looked at the other guys we had, pitchers like Eric Plunk and Jose Rijo, you knew it was a good mix and that we had some-thing special coming. These were guys who were going to excel."

In McGwire's first month at Triple A, he hit .344, hitting in 20 of his first 21 games. He did even better in July, raising his average to .351 whle hitting nine homers and driving in 29 runs. His average dropped off in August, but through August 20 his combined totals at Huntsville and Tacoma were a .311 average, 23 homers, and 112 RBIs. He also had commited 41 errors, but the A's were willing to accept those learning mistakes.

He was still working on the defense, fielding as many as 250 grounders a day from Lieppman. Lieppman had even gotten him a special glove to practice with, a small Joe Morgan model, figuring if he could catch the ball using that glove, it would be even easier when he switched back to a regular-size model. In his first 28 games at Tacoma, McGwire made 14 errors. In his final 50 games at Tacoma, he committed only 11 errors.

Lieppman's work with McGwire was interrupted on August 20, for a very good reason. Lieppman told McGwire that day that he was on his way to the major leagues.

That news prompted McGwire to reflect, for a moment, on his decision five years earlier to accept the USC scholarship instead of signing with the Expos out of high school. What would have happened to him had he made the opposite decision?

"Who knows?" he said. "I might be pitching for the Expos, or I might be washing cars."

6

A MAJOR LEAGUER

McGwire joined the A's in Baltimore and got quite an introduction to the major leagues. His first two games in an Oakland uniform were rained out.

He was added to the roster to replace second baseman Tony Phillips, who had been placed on the disabled list with a strained knee. The opening night rainout was to be made up as part of a twi-night doubleheader the following day, and McGwire was set to make his major-league debut against the Orioles' Mike Flanagan.

Rain wiped out the doubleheader as well, however, and the A's moved on to New York. On Friday night, August 22, 1986, McGwire's name appeared in the A's starting lineup, batting seventh, playing third base, as the Yankees started Dennis Rasmussen on the mound.

Before the game, McGwire did what any new tourist would do—he went and saw the sights.

As he walked out of the visiting dugout at Yankee Stadium, McGwire headed past center field to Monument Park, the home of bronze plaques commemorating the greatest players in Yankees history, including Roger Maris.

"The first thing I did was come look at the plaques," McGwire said.

McGwire admits he never was much of a student of baseball history as a youngster, but this was a moment he couldn't pass up. He knows he was drawn there for a special reason, but at the time he didn't know what it was.

There was nothing special about McGwire's first game in the majors. He went 0-for-3 as the A's lost 3–2.

He did manage to get his name in the game story the following morning in *The New York Times*, although for a negative reason. He had cut off a throw from left fielder Jose Canseco toward the plate in the fourth inning, allowing the Yankees to score the tying run, when the throw might have reached the plate in time to retire the runner.

"As soon as I did it, I knew I shouldn't have," McGwire said.

New manager Tony La Russa, who had taken over the A's on July 1, was willing to overlook rookie mistakes of aggression, however, and McGwire was back in the lineup in the same spot the next night. He again went 0-for-3, but this time the A's won 2–1 as Canseco broke out of an 0-for-40 slump with an RBI double in the ninth inning. McGwire did hit some long fly balls that were tracked down in the outfield.

McGwire was in the sixth spot in the order for his third game in the majors, a Sunday afternoon contest against the Yankees, on August 24, and a familiar face was on the mound for New York. Tommy John was pitching for the Yankees, the same Tommy John who four years earlier had pitched for the Angels . . . and become a dental patient of Dr. John McGwire, Mark's father.

Mark and John had once been paired in a celebrity golf outing, and when John was traded to the Angels in 1982 and needed a dentist he looked up Dr. McGwire.

John said the elder McGwire always talked about his son and what a good baseball player he was, but he only half-listened. "I thought he was just bragging," John said. He got a firsthand education on this day, as McGwire collected the first three hits of his major-league career in Oakland's 11–4 win.

McGwire's first two hits came off John, including a run-scoring double in the sixth inning. As the A's headed for the next stop on their road trip, Detroit, McGwire finally had a reason to smile.

He was smiling even more the next night. Batting against Walt Terrell in the fifth inning, McGwire launched the first homer of his major-league career, a shot over the center field wall estimated at 450 feet.

That blast gave La Russa and the rest of the A's an idea what they could expect in the future. McGwire finished the year with three homers but hit just .189 and commited six errors in 18 games. The organization, wanting him to continue working every day in the winter, asked him to play winter ball at Licey in the Dominican Republic, where Lieppman, his manager at Triple A Tacoma, was going to be the manager.

McGwire agreed to go, but he wasn't happy about it. He lasted about a month before he gave up and went home. That didn't make the A's happy.

"He and Steinbach and Nelson all went down there, but from the very beginning Mark did not enjoy playing ball there," Lieppman said. "He wore it very openly that it wasn't going to help him. He lasted about a month."

McGwire admits he had a bad attitude toward playing in the Dominican Republic even before he got there. He blamed it mostly on some bad experiences when he had been on the Pan-American team that played in Venezuela a few years earlier.

"The villages we lived in were not completed," McGwire said of his exposure to Latin America. "The dormitories were filthy dirty. The sheets were dirty. The toilet paper would get wet so there was no toilet paper. One thing that really saved me is they had phones. I called home every day."

Even the phones were not enough to convince him to stay in the Dominican Republic, however.

"When you're in a country like that, you can't eat

the way you're used to, the customs are different, everything is strange," McGwire said. "I couldn't concentrate on my game and I wasn't hitting. It just wasn't helping me at all, so I told the A's I was coming home."

Many people in the organization thought McGwire was making a bad career move. Nelson was still well liked by the organization, and the team had added a veteran over the winter in Ron Cey, who could platoon with Carney Lansford at either first or third.

"There were some circles that believed if Nelson had any kind of spring training at all, that he was more commited and had given a better effort," Lieppman said. "Mark's stock had gone down because of that."

McGwire never believed that, and he didn't think his spot on the major-league club would be determined by what happened over the winter in the Dominican Republic. He prepared himself for spring training in Arizona, convinced that a good performance there would keep him in the major leagues.

7

ROOKIE OF THE YEAR

A s McGwire reported to the A's spring training facility in Scottsdale, Arizona, he knew his decision to come home early from the Dominican Republic had not earned him any points with the team's hierarchy. Still, his opinion was that if he played well enough during the spring, he could force GM Sandy Alderson and manager Tony La Russa to overlook that action and have no choice but to keep him on the major-league roster.

Reggie Jackson had re-signed with the A's as a free agent over the winter, after five years with the Angels, and he came to camp trying to prove that at age 40 he still could be an effective player.

"He worked as hard as Reggie," La Russa said of McGwire's spring. "Reggie had set a goal for himself to work harder than anybody in camp, and Mark stayed right with him. That's when I knew we had something special."

In the spring games, McGwire hit .322 and led the A's with 23 RBIs. He made the team, as did his fellow rookie Rob Nelson, who also played well in the spring. La Russa's plan as the regular season began was to have them share playing time at first base, while also giving some at-bats to Lansford and Ron Cey.

"Tony told me I'd probably just be playing against left-handers for a while and I told him that was fine," McGwire said. "I told him I'd just keep working hard and be ready whenever he needed me."

Neither McGwire nor Nelson got off to a quick start, however. Nelson struck out in 12 of his first 24 at bats. Through April 19, McGwire wasn't doing much better, hitting .167 with one homer.

La Russa could see his idea of keeping both players on the roster wasn't helping either of them, so he made a decision. Even though McGwire wasn't getting many hits, La Russa thought he was swinging better, so he gave the everyday first base assignment to McGwire and told Nelson he was going back to Tacoma. La Russa also told McGwire he was moving back to his natural position of first base.

McGwire didn't exactly respond to the move with cartwheels. He went 0-for-4 on April 20, dropping his average to .136.

He did, however, hit his second homer of the season the following day against the Angels in Anaheim, and as he began to play on a regular basis his confidence grew and so did his average and home run total. He also felt more comfortable being back at first base, which allowed him to use more of his preparation time before a game batting instead of working on his defense.

"I don't think it's possible to really show what you can do unless you're playing every day," McGwire said. "It takes that to get in rhythm with your swing. I wanted to have that opportunity, and once I got it, I wanted to make the most of it."

McGwire finished April with four homers, but no one—McGwire, La Russa, or anybody else—was prepared for what was to come in May.

In a three-game series in Detroit, May 8–10, McGwire hit five homers. In a 16-game span, he hit 11 homers. He finished the month of May with 15, only one less than the major-league record for most homers hit in that month, 16, set by Mickey Mantle in 1956.

McGwire took over the league lead in homers and suddenly became a hot topic for reporters and other baseball personnel as well. He couldn't understand what all the excitement was about. He was quietly getting dressed in his locker after the home run burst in Detroit when he turned around and found several reporters standing next to him.

"What's going on?" he said in a startled voice, wondering if the reporters were there to deliver some bad news. "You guys all want to talk to me?"

Being a media celebrity was exciting for Mc-

Gwire, but he wasn't the type of player to capitalize on his sudden fame and get his picture on the cover of every national sports publication. He was pleasant to reporters, answering their questions, and often even ended interviews with a polite "thank you," something almost unheard-of in most baseball circles.

More than once he apologized for not having anything exciting to say and not offering comments that overwhelmed reporters. When McGwire was asked the reason for his success and sudden home run spurt, a typical answer was, "I can't explain why they're happening. It's just feeling more relaxed, seeing it, and hitting it."

What was hard for McGwire then is still hard today—he doesn't enjoy talking about himself, and he doesn't enjoy being the star of the show. He wants to be part of a team, to be treated the same and receive the same reception as everybody else.

That attitude quickly earned him praise and support from veterans on the A's and throughout baseball, who admired that characteristic and the fact that he didn't try to be the star.

"For three months there wasn't a time when I came to the park that there wasn't somebody waiting for me at my locker," McGwire said. "I like to get out to the park early and kick back for a while before I really start thinking about the game. I had no chance to do that. There would always be at least one person there, if not to do a story, just to talk to me for a while."

It helped McGwire that he had a player like Jackson on his team, both to give advice and to watch how he dealt with the media.

"The thing I like about him is his makeup," Jackson said at the time. "He's never too high or too low. He's the same every day."

When the A's went to New York at the end of May, he was told there were some reporters who wanted to talk with him. He thought there would be one or two writers present, but instead he found himself in front of 30 people with notebooks, tape recorders, and cameras.

"This is all a surprise to me," McGwire said.

What may have helped McGwire to relax a little was on the final day of the three-game series in New York, on May 31, when he looked out to the mound he saw his dad's old patient, Tommy John, staring back at him.

McGwire hit John's first pitch of the second inning deep into the right field stands. After grounding out in the fourth, he led off the seventh by sending a 1–0 pitch well beyond the center field fence.

John was able to laugh about the homers, since he and the Yankees won the game 9–5. Opening his mouth for reporters, he said, "You see all that? I've got $6,000 worth of gold in there, and it's all in Mark's father's pocket."

When told of John's remark, Dr. McGwire said, "Tell him I owe him a free cleaning. One for each home run.

"I used to needle Tommy a little bit," the elder

McGwire continued. "I would start asking Tommy how he was going to pitch Mark, and he'd always say, 'Down and away.' "

The sudden home run pace prompted comparisons to other home run hitters of the past and was the first time McGwire's name had been linked in the same sentence with those of Babe Ruth and Roger Maris.

The attention forced McGwire and his roommate on the road, rookie catcher Terry Steinbach, to put a hold on the telephone calls to their room. McGwire didn't like the talk and projections about home run records then any more than he does now.

"Mark is very pleased about what he's accomplished, but as far as being carried away or caught up in all that talk about Roger Maris, he keeps it in perspective," Steinbach said then. "We'll talk about game situations and how we're being pitched, but he's very realistic. When he was hitting a home run every seven at-bats and people were saying he'd hit 70, he was saying, 'Forget it. Don't be ridiculous.' "

McGwire did have a different home run record to shoot for—the rookie mark of 38 that had been set by Wally Berger of the Boston Braves in 1930 and matched by Frank Robinson of the Reds in 1956. The AL mark for most homers by a rookie was 37, set by the Indians' Al Rosen in 1950.

Berger, eighty-one years old when McGwire made his bid for the record and living in Manhattan Beach, California, was getting more attention and notice from reporters than he had when he was playing.

When reporters called, Berger usually had the same message that he asked them to pass along to McGwire. "Just wish that young man luck," Berger said. "Tell him I hope he hits 60. Tell him I hope he hits 61, and let everybody try to chase that one for a while.

"I'll be glad when he breaks the record. Then I won't have guys breathing down my neck anymore."

During a game in Cleveland on June 27, McGwire put on an amazing display—homering three times. In the series, he hit five homers and scored runs on nine consecutive at-bats. The five homers increased his season total to 27 and tied the record for most homers in two consecutive games.

"I don't know how many hits he had," said Cleveland catcher Chris Bando. "I stopped counting. He hit four or five different pitches. He hit fastballs. He hit curveballs. He hit sliders. He hit forkballs. You've got to hand it to him; he hit everything."

After the fifth homer, Bando was in shock. As he came up to bat, Carney Lansford said, Bando told him, "Forget it. I'm telling him [McGwire] the pitch. It doesn't matter."

McGwire's teammates couldn't decide on the best nickname for him. Big Mac was too obvious, and so were the ones that called attention to his red hair—Agent Orange and Orange Crush.

His teammates also didn't let McGwire forget there were other skills he needed to work on. Said Jackson, "He needs a better home run trot." Added Lansford, "He needs a better handshake."

McGwire's homer total reached 33 when he hit

two blasts on July 11 against Milwaukee, two days before the break for the All-Star game, which, coincidentally, was being played in Oakland that year.

An indication that McGwire was going to do some damage in the game came during batting practice, when a line drive off McGwire's bat broke the left wrist of teammate Tony Phillips.

When his second homer against Milwaukee turned a 5–4 deficit into a 6–5 lead in the eighth inning, Jackson made McGwire step out of the dugout for the first curtain call of his career.

"Reggie was the one who told me to go out and tip my cap," McGwire said. "He's one who knows a lot about those kind of things. My wife was here and she didn't even see me."

McGwire's wife, Kathy, was enjoying her husband's success as much as he was. The couple had met at a preseason baseball party at USC, where she was one of the team's bat girls, and shortly before the 1987 season began she had learned she was pregnant with their first child.

McGwire always had been protective of his privacy and enjoyed quiet evenings at home instead of becoming part of the party scene, and he found home to be his retreat from the attention his on-field success was attracting.

"We watch a lot of TV," McGwire said of his activities away from the ballpark.

If he had been watching *Fantasy Island*, maybe he could have found an explanation for his sudden success and how in three months he had gone from a rookie hoping to play well enough to stick in the major leagues to a national celebrity.

McGwire was named to the All-Star team as a reserve by Boston manager John McNamara, even though he had not been listed on the ballot at the start of the season. When turning in to the American League the players from their squad to be listed, the A's had put Nelson's name at first base instead of Mc-Gwire's.

"*Weird*'s not the word," McGwire said. "It's *incredible*. No way did I ever picture myself in this situation, being an All-Star. I don't know how to feel, how to accept it."

Said Steinbach, "Any player having the kind of year he is, I think it would have to have some effect, no matter who you are. But with Mac, I can't tell any difference from the first week he became a regular player until now. We joke around, just like we did before. It's not like he doesn't have time for anybody anymore. He's just being as normal as he's always been."

McGwire's friends tried to do their part to make certain he didn't get bigheaded and caught up in his success—like the time McGwire and Jackson were being interviewed together on NBC-TV.

"I was talking and Mark was intent on looking at me and listening," Jackson said. "Steinbach came up behind Mark and put a big cream pie right in his face. The thing was, the TV interview never stopped. Mark wiped off as much of the pie as he could, but for the rest of the interview he had cream all over his face."

The A's tried to help McGwire enjoy the All-Star experience by allowing him to do only one mass interview with the media and cutting off questions after 15 minutes. McGwire asked for and received special introductions to Joe DiMaggio and Willie Mays. He met many of the National League stars he had only seen on television, including Mike Schmidt and Dale Murphy.

Perhaps still a bit overwhelmed, McGwire entered the game as a sub for elected first baseman Don Mattingly but went 0-for-3.

As the second half of the season began and talk about McGwire chasing the various home run records again heated up, he had to look no farther than across the locker room, toward Jackson, to know what happens in the first half of the season isn't always matched by what happens the rest of the year. In 1969, everybody had been talking about Jackson. He had 37 homers at the All-Star break, the most ever, but proceeded to hit only 10 more during the rest of the season and finished at 47. He had come down with hives and had to come out of the lineup.

Jackson was glad he was there to help McGwire in any way he could, but he knew that whether or not McGwire continued to hit homers was up to nobody but himself.

"There really wasn't much I could tell him," Jackson said. "I certainly wasn't going to tell him how to swing the bat. The big thing was to give him a pat on the back when he was going bad. He didn't need me to say anything when he was going good, but if he was having a hard time, I'd just tell him to keep swinging and he'd be OK.

"As a matter of fact, there was one time when he'd gone a couple of weeks without a home run and I told him I was impressed because he was still running as hard and playing as hard as when he was hot. There aren't many players who can do that."

Said McGwire, "Reggie has been a great help. Going into spring training, I didn't know what kind of a person he was, but he motivates a player. Just watch the way he hustles. It's a tribute to him at age 40. I've always hustled, but watching Reggie makes you want to play harder."

McGwire finished July with 37 homers, tying Rosen's AL rookie record. He tied the major-league mark with a homer off Mike Moore at Seattle on August 11, then broke the record three days later with a homer off Don Sutton of the Angels at California.

The clubhouse attendants had a bottle of champagne waiting for McGwire after the game, and reporters were assembled in an interview room. After the public functions were complete, however, McGwire had his own private celebration.

"I went back to my hotel room, got something to eat, and went to bed," he said.

McGwire hit only one more homer in the month, however, and looking back, he believes the media pressure was a big reason for his power drop-off.

"It bothered me," McGwire admitted in an interview with *Inside Sports* following the end of the 1987 season. "It affected my concentration because I couldn't get in the right frame of mind. I had never thought much about records, but there was always somebody there to remind me of them. First it was the rookie home run record, and then it was Ruth and Maris. It put pressure on me that I hadn't been putting on myself. I had a bad August, and I know that was the reason."

The other reason, of course, was that he was no longer a secret. Pitchers were aware of him, as were the advance scouts, and strategies were adopted to try to retire McGwire and not leave the ball over the plate, where he could drive it over the wall.

"They'd make sure that, if they [the pitchers] missed, they weren't missing over the plate," Mc-Gwire said. "A pitch would be two feet inside or two feet outside. The word got around that I was a first-ball hitter, so I didn't see anything good on the first pitch. I had to learn patience. But that's part of hitting. Pitchers adjust to hitters, and hitters have to adjust to pitchers."

Normally, however, those adjustments aren't made under the microscope of the national media.

"After a while, it got ridiculous," McGwire said in the same interview. "Guys were asking me questions and expecting the kind of answers they'd get from a veteran. I remember after one game we lost, a guy tried to get me to explain why we'd lost. I said, 'Hey, I'm just a rookie. I'm just 23 years old. I can't explain something like that.' He kept bugging me, so I finally said I wasn't going to answer any more questions.

"The next day, I see a story, I think it was an AP story, that said, 'Pressure Getting to McGwire.' I can laugh about it now, but it wasn't so funny then."

About the only safe zone in public McGwire had away from reporters was when he was on the field playing. He tried to calm himself down and stay relaxed in the same manner he had displayed since his days in Little League.

"I play this game like a kid," McGwire said in an interview in August 1987. "I talk to myself in the on-deck circle and I try to mimic the announcer to keep myself amused. This game will drive you crazy if you let it, but the veterans joke with me all the time and keep me loose. I never have had a lot of time to think about the things I've done."

Even the way he handled the negative times was impressive to veteran baseball people around him.

"You've got to be impressed by his size, by the way he stands at the plate, by his power and ability to hit the breaking pitch," said Oakland's third base coach that season, Jim Lefebvre. "But what I like most is his makeup. He's very mature for his age. He reminds me of Steve Garvey. Garv could strike out three times or have a great day and be the same. He just walked in and went about his business."

Cey, who actually was released by the A's in July in part because of McGwire's success, nonetheless offered some compliments for McGwire.

"I like his attitude," Cey said. "That's what's separating him from somebody else. He has basically an attitude of what you'd hope a veteran player develops in time—that you accept the highs and lows as basically the same thing.

"Mark's basically a low-key, down-to-earth guy. There's not a lot of flare there. Talent-wise, he has the makeup to be a big home run hitter. But I don't think he's got the personality that's going to dictate a lot of attention. And to be quite honest, I think that's good."

McGwire's former teammate at Modesto Walt Weiss was called up in September, and he was amazed at how little had changed about McGwire despite his success and sudden fame.

"He's just an easygoing, down-to-earth guy who wants to go out and play and doesn't like all the attention," Weiss said. "Not much has changed about him, even now. He would rather not be in the limelight. Everybody else changed around him, but he didn't change."

The A's rookie sensation from the previous year, Jose Canseco, always was a little more flamboyant and outgoing than McGwire. They quickly became known as the "Bash Brothers," a marketing concept that took off in the Bay Area and across the country.

Canseco, who had won the Rookie of the Year award in 1986 after hitting 33 homers, followed up with 31 in 1987. He was able to give McGwire advice, as Jackson did, but the two of them were never as close as the advertising concept would suggest.

"I get it all the time, 'Where's Jose? Where's your Bash Brother?' " McGwire said. Added Canseco, "People think we're hooked at the waist."

Canseco developed a reputation of being much

more outspoken than McGwire and was known for living his life at a little faster pace away from the ballpark. While they rarely were together away from the ballpark, they did often communicate during the games.

"Jose and I always are talking to each other," McGwire said. "We just go out and play our own game. We always get each other motivated. If we don't have any hits going into our last at-bats, we'll always pump each other up."

Canseco was more than slightly impressed with McGwire's performance on the field and the way he conducted himself off the field.

"I'd say the only thing he really lacks is speed," Canseco said. "But most power hitters, you know, all they need is jogging speed to go around the bases anyway. He's a real good breaking-ball hitter. He's got a good extension on his swing. He's going to hit a lot of home runs, no doubt in my mind."

As he struggled through August, McGwire finally decided to regain control over his time when he was at the ballpark. He still tried to be polite, but he learned to say no, that he couldn't fulfill every interview request. He began to spend more time in the trainer's room, not because he was injured but because it was off-limits to the press.

Even some of the reporters admitted they thought the coverage was getting a little carried away. One unidentified reporter told *The New York Times* in August, "We've done everything except interview his dog."

Frank Blackman wrote in the *San Francisco Examiner* on July 19: "The only American more intriguing than Mark McGwire this summer is Ollie North, another slugger famed for his ability to hit from the right side."

La Russa thought that finally getting the rookie record might allow McGwire to relax a little and stop the media crush, but there still were other records to break and reporters with questions. La Russa remained pleased with the way McGwire handled the entire situation.

"I've been impressed since the first day of spring training," La Russa said, "He came there and had to play his way on the team and he's earned everything he's gotten. He's got good ability and he's kept his wits about him. He's got a chance to be a very productive hitter because he uses the whole field.

"He's got a very compact stroke, the ball jumps off his bat, and, if he keeps applying himself, he's got a lot of ways to drive in a run. There's a lot of pitches he can handle. You can't stack the defense against him. You can't pitch him one way."

McGwire hit his 40th homer on August 29, at Toronto. A day later, Nelson—the player McGwire had begun the season platooning with—was traded off of Tacoma's roster with pitcher Dave Leiper to San Diego for pitcher Storm Davis.

While McGwire had been making national headlines, Nelson had undergone a disappointing season. Hoping like McGwire to make the A's in April, he had instead been relegated to Tacoma and hit a career low

.215. He did hit 20 homers, but nine of them came in the final month of the season.

Unfortunately for Nelson, the move to San Diego did not produce any better career results. He played in 10 games for the Padres at the end of the 1987 season and spent almost all of 1988 at Triple A Las Vegas (hitting 23 homers) before playing seven games in San Diego at the end of the season. He did hit his one and only major-league homer before his last chance of making the majors evaporated.

"It was certainly a unique situation, with them starting out so equal and then one doing so well and the other falling off the bandwagon completely," said Grady Fuson, the Oakland scout. "Usually you know a little better than that.

"Rob hung around for a few years but basically just turned into a Triple A kind of guy. He always had power, but he never became a good hitter."

As McGwire began September, the questions about chasing the ghosts of Maris and Ruth finally died off, but there still was one additional homer record in sight—Jackson's Oakland mark of 47, set in 1969.

A two-homer game at Texas on September 15 increased McGwire's season total to 45, and after hitting number 46 at Kansas City on September 20 he came home for the start of a four-game series against the White Sox on September 24. His blast that day tied Jackson's mark, and he didn't have long to wait for the record breaker, connecting the following day off White Sox reliever Bobby Thigpen. The blast also enabled McGwire to break Jackson's team mark for most total bases in a season.

With eight games to play, now the talk was whether McGwire could become only the 11th player in history, and the first rookie, to hit 50 homers in a season. He hit number 49 on September 29 against Cleveland. There were five games remaining.

After two homerless games, he left with the rest of the A's for the final three games of the season, in Chicago.

His wife, Kathy, was expecting the couple's first child at any time, and McGwire already had made up his mind that he was coming home the minute he learned she had gone into labor. For the first two games in Chicago nothing happened—he didn't hit a homer, and Kathy didn't go into labor.

Early in the morning of October 4, the final day of the season, McGwire was awakened in his hotel room by a telephone call. Kathy was on her way to the hospital. He called La Russa and told his manager that he was leaving.

McGwire caught the first plane back to California and reached the hospital forty-five minutes before Matthew was born. Later, McGwire was told that the wind was blowing out that day at Comiskey Park and that he might have gotten that elusive 50th homer.

Kathy McGwire said she and her husband had discussed in advance whether he would come home or stay with the team and she left the decision up to him.

"I wouldn't be alone," she said. "My parents live

four blocks away and this is their first grandchild, so they were at the hospital with me."

McGwire said, "It wasn't a tough decision to make. As long as the club was in contention, I was staying, but we were out of the race that last week. I talked it over with Tony [La Russa], who's a real family man himself, and he told me it was really important to be there for the first one."

McGwire had no regrets. Being there for Matthew's birth, he said, was his 50th homer..

The year had begun with McGwire being a platoon player. It ended with McGwire's total of 49 homers equaling the Cubs' Andre Dawson for the major-league lead. He became the first rookie to lead the majors or tie for the lead since Brooklyn's Tim Jordan did it in 1906. His total of 118 RBIs was the most by a rookie in the majors since Walt Dropo drove in 144 for the Red Sox in 1950.

Even though there were other good rookies in the American League in 1987, including Kevin Seitzer of the Royals, Matt Nokes of Detroit, Mike Greenwell of Boston, and Devon White in California, there was little suspense when the voting totals were announced for the Baseball Writers' Rookie of the Year award. McGwire was a unanimous selection, voted first on all 28 ballots, submitted by two writers in each of the 14 American League cities.

McGwire was only the second unanimous selection since the award began in 1949, joining Boston catcher Carlton Fisk, who won it in 1972.

"A lot of people kept drilling it in my head:

'There's no way you're going to lose,' " McGwire said. "I was introduced at a golf tournament as the hands-down winner of the Rookie of the Year award. I don't like that, but you have to deal with it. You need to put it out of your mind."

McGwire received enough votes to finish sixth in the balloting for the league's Most Valuable Player award.

Kathy McGwire said one of the reasons she thought her husband had enjoyed such a successful season was that he was able to put matters like awards and the media pressure out of his mind.

"Mark keeps on an even keel," she said. "He doesn't let anything change him. He won't overextend himself. He's Mark. He'll still take out the trash and wash the cars."

Along with those off-season activities, McGwire had more time to reflect on what an amazing season he had enjoyed. He thought about some of the other monster years enjoyed by great players in the past, such as the years George Brett and Rod Carew had pursued a .400 batting average, and wondered if fewer distractions would have helped those players to reach that goal.

When Matthew was born, McGwire said he was his 50th homer—that there would be other chances to hit 50 in a season. Still, that winter, as he sat at home in his apartment in Costa Mesa, California, he had moments of doubt. After all, 50 home runs had only been reached 10 times in baseball history. What evidence was there to think he was going to have a better year than he had enjoyed in 1987?

And if he did happen to get close to Maris's and Ruth's record home run totals, would the media pressure be too much for him?

"What I dealt with was tremendous," he said that winter. "In a way it was good because now I know better how to deal with it. It's pretty difficult. It reminded me when George Brett was close to hitting .400. If the press let him alone and didn't need to ask every day, 'Are you going to get a hit?,' if they had just let him play, I think he would have hit .400.

"It does come with the territory, but you have to ask yourself what would happen if they let the guy alone. If someone does break the 61 barrier, it would be quite an accomplishment."

Even before he set foot on the practice field in Arizona for the start of spring training, McGwire knew he was going to be under more media pressure as the 1988 season began. Could he repeat his success or was he a one-year wonder? He knew that if his home run total fell, some critics would be saying he had a disappointing year. If McGwire thought he was under pressure before, he was in for a new feeling in his sophomore season.

"The only thing I can do is go out and play hard every day, like I started doing in spring training this year," McGwire said. "That's the only thing I can ask of myself."

8

A WINNING TEAM

About the only part of McGwire's 1987 season that he had not been pleased with was the A's final record. Oakland entered September only one and a half games out of first place, before fading back to .500 and a third-place finish in the American League West.

Even though McGwire had a strong personal September, he vowed to work harder over the winter in the weight room to try to increase his strength and better enable him to withstand the rigors of the 162-game season.

When he reported to spring training in late February, the *San Francisco Chronicle* reported that McGwire had indeed bulked up.

"I've been really serious about this for two

years," McGwire said of his weight-lifting routine. "I hit the gym from day one at the end of the season last year. It's what keeps me going. I want to be even bigger than I am now."

The *Chronicle* reported: "Besides time in the weightroom, McGwire is counting on a program of dietary supplements to help him keep his strength during the year. The top of his locker resembles a health food store with jars of vitamins, amino acids, and something called 'Sudden Impact.' That isn't McGwire hitting the ball, but rather a drink of anabolic ingredients similar to steroids without the nasty side effects."

McGwire told the newspaper, "I have just been taking it the last couple of months. It has done me a lot of good."

With any professional athlete, feeling good physically contributes in large measure to how the athlete feels about himself mentally. If he is mentally sound, he is going to be a confident player, which is going to translate into positive results on the field. It took McGwire a while to realize that the weight lifting he did was going to raise his inner level of confidence and make him a better player.

Only the most optimistic fans could have believed that McGwire would improve on the performance of his rookie year. The A's tried to downplay the talk that he would do better, and even though McGwire knew such talk was coming, he tried to predict in spring training that he probably would not hit as many homers or drive in as many runs.

"Everybody is going to bring up the sophomore slump," he said. "You can't worry about it. All you can do is go out and let your ability take care of what you are capable of doing.

"I set a real high precedent. But I don't set goals. I'll just go out and do what I can do, and the home runs will fall into place. I'm not going to change anything."

McGwire has never been the kind of player who tries to get too analytical about his performance. The simpler he keeps the concept of hitting, the better he seems to do. La Russa and the A's coaches encouraged him to do exactly that.

"I just like to go out and play baseball and not think about the technical part of it," McGwire said. "When you start thinking about it, you start screwing yourself up. I just go out there and let my ability take care of it."

Bob Watson, who had worked with McGwire in the minors and as the A's hitting coach in 1987, tried to warn people not to expect McGwire to hit 49 homers again.

"If he has quality at-bats, the home runs will come," Watson said. "But the fans and the media can't be too harsh on him. If he hits 30 home runs, that's still a great year. Reggie [Jackson] hit 47 his second year and didn't come close again. Yet he had some great years."

Watson also knew that the supporting cast for McGwire had changed. Jackson was gone, but the team had added two veteran sluggers in Dave Parker and Don Baylor. Both were players McGwire could learn from, the A's believed.

Before the team left spring training, McGwire gave the fans and everybody else at Scottsdale Stadium, the spring training home of the Giants, something to talk about. McGwire hit a ball that cleared a 30-foot-high wall 430 feet from home plate. The ball struck a 40-foot palm tree planted 20 feet beyond the wall.

The ball was hit so high that San Francisco shortstop Jose Uribe broke back on the ball, thinking he had a chance to catch it. Center fielder Brett Butler knew better, and turned around and just watched where it landed.

Even though he has said he doesn't try to think too much about his hitting, there is no doubt McGwire would remember exactly who was pitching when he hit that towering homer, what kind of pitch he hit, and where the pitch was thrown. He doesn't keep a computerized record of those things, as do some hitters. He keeps it in his head.

"I don't like writing things down," he said. "I know a pitcher by warm-ups. If he can warm up, by the way he's throwing in the bullpen I don't need to know his name. I remember what he does—if I got a hit off him or he got me out."

A few days into the regular season, McGwire had another reason to remember some pitchers. All of a sudden, perhaps in an attempt at intimidation, pitchers were throwing at him. More specifically, they were throwing at his head.

On April 11, when he was beaned by California's Kirk McCaskill on an 0-2 pitch, McGwire finally had enough. Although he didn't charge the mound and instigate a brawl, he did take several steps toward McCaskill and threw up his arms, a universal gesture for, "What the heck's going on?"

Since he had come up to the majors in August 1986, McGwire had been hit by pitches seven times. He wanted it stopped.

McCaskill, of course, said he didn't intend to hit McGwire. It was merely a coincidence that the pitch followed a McGwire home run in his previous at-bat and an aggressive swing on the previous pitch.

Some of his teammates were ready to brawl, as they had been the previous year when McGwire was hit by Wes Gardner of the Red Sox. Reggie Jackson was ready to charge out of the dugout, but stopped when McGwire calmly trotted to first.

"The man who gets hit has to start it," Jackson said.

McGwire didn't want to start something; he wanted to stop the pitches at his head.

"I wanted to know what was going on," McGwire said. "Fourth game of the season and somebody already is hit in the head. I've only been in the league one year and four days and I've already been hit twice in the skull.

"I'm tired of it. I think a lot of people are tired of it. You throw a baseball at somebody's head and you could end their career."

If McCaskill had thrown a pitch at either Baylor

or Parker, he would have had a brawl on his hands. Said Baylor, "Hit in the head? I'm out of the game [for fighting] and the pitcher's out of the game, too [ejected or injured]."

Added Parker, "I wouldn't tolerate that, and you don't in the National League because those guys [pitchers] have to go to the plate. Those guys gotta learn that being in the AL and having the DH [designated hitter] doesn't give them the license to do that kind of crap.

"He [McGwire] and I come from different backgrounds. I was a street-fightin' guy, had that reputation, and maybe that helped when I was a young player."

Baylor, who holds the career record for most times hit by a pitch, was glad McGwire got upset.

"You can't just stand there and say, 'I'm putting you on warning,' because impressions don't take care of it," Baylor said. "You have to go beyond that. You have to take the next step."

Karl Kuehl believed at the time that McGwire's reaction actually improved his batting ability. It made him mad, which prompted him to change where he stood in the batter's box.

"I think he just made up his mind that the pitchers were not going to run him out of the league," Kuehl said. "He moved up closer to the plate, almost daring the pitchers to hit him, and that made him a better hitter."

Despite responding to that challenge and making what the A's considered a positive response, Mc-

Gwire, as expected, was finding it hard to keep up his home run pace from 1987.

At the All-Star break, he had hit 16 homers, less than half his total of the previous year. He had only two homers and seven RBIs in June, and his season average fell to .236. Based on what he had accomplished the previous year, however, he was voted the starting first baseman for the AL for the All-Star game, in Cincinnati, and there he collected his first All-Star hit.

As the media pressure from hitting home runs had gotten to McGwire a year earlier, this time he was suffering from expectations others had placed on him.

"People say they don't expect me to hit 49 home runs again, but they do," McGwire said. "I know people will always look at me differently because of that. They expect me to have 33 homers at the All-Star break. Give me a break."

Dealing with those expectations of others did, however, teach McGwire a valuable lesson: if he couldn't control what other people said or thought, there was no sense in worrying about it or trying to react to it.

"I used to worry about what people thought about me, but I don't anymore," he said. "What's important is what I do, not what somebody else thinks of it. I know that no matter what I do, somebody is going to think I should have done better, so I can't let that bother me."

McGwire and his teammates weren't so sure

about their thoughts when La Russa decided that it was important to act and dress professionally off the field, so the team instituted a dress code for most out-of-town trips, calling for identical gray herringbone blazers. McGwire wasn't crazy about the idea, and someone at Chicago's Midway Airport saw the group and said, "Oh, they must be the band."

"It was Tony's idea, but it didn't sit real well with everybody," said pitcher Rick Honeycutt. "Guys started 'wearing' them by draping them over their arm, or they were wadding them up in their brief-cases. Mark hated it. We really did kind of look like a band or a college team."

The spectacle of the sport coats served to distract McGwire's attention at odd moments during the season, but most of his thoughts still were focused on what was, or wasn't, happening on the field. San Francisco columnist Art Spander wrote that Mc-Gwire had made a mistake during his rookie season—he played too well. "In 1988, what you read about Mark McGwire is not what he's doing but what he's not. No wonder ballplayers get frustrated," Spander wrote.

McGwire told Spander, "I'm tired of people comparing this year with last year. Every baseball person I talk to would like to have 19 home runs and 62 RBIs [in early August].

"People think I'm not swinging the bat. But I'm swinging pretty well. Those pitchers are tough on me. They're tough on the A's. We're in first place, and they never let up against us. They show us their best stuff. They show me their best stuff. It's a lot of work."

Two pitchers McGwire found particularly tough to hit were Ron Guidry of the Yankees and Tom Henke of the Blue Jays.

"I always walk back to the dugout against those guys," McGwire said. "I think I've got one hit and the rest strikeouts aganst Guidry, and I've struck out every time up against Henke. Guidry's got the best left-handed slider of anyone I've ever seen, and Henke just always pitches me tough."

The people around McGwire could see the mental strain he was under, just as he was under a different kind of pressure the year before.

"I think Mark found out that the second year is probably the toughest year," said Oakland coach Jim Lefebvre. "It's not only the pitchers pitching him a little more carefully from the get-go. It's the whole scene. The fans expecting so much from him. The press expecting so much from him.

"Now people have something to compare him to. Mark says it doesn't bother him. But inside, I believe he's sensitive to that. He figures if he jacks a couple out, people might start leaving him alone. But it's when he starts swinging for the fences that he has most of his problems."

McGwire tried to concentrate on other parts of his game during the season, like improving his defense, as a way to keep his mind off not playing as well as he would have liked offensively. He and Carney Lansford held daily contests to see who could field the most ground balls during batting practice.

"If you really want to see a guy who's into the

game, one who's really disciplined, watch his defense," Lefebvre said. "Sometimes a guy will go 0-for-4 or 0-for-a-couple-of-days and it affects his defense. Mark's not that way. He goes out on the field and regardless of whether he hits a home run, strikes out, or hits into a double play, he concentrates on his defense. That is a big factor in the development and maturing of a ballplayer."

Despite his personal year not going as well as he had hoped, McGwire was able to find consolation in the play of the team. The A's moved into first place on April 20 and stayed there the rest of the season. They were nine games in front going into September and coasted to the division championship, finishing with 104 victories.

McGwire finished the season with more-than-respectable numbers—32 homers, the third-highest total in the league, and 99 RBIs. He might have gotten the 100th RBI had he not missed seven of the A's final 16 games because of stiffness in his lower back.

The national spotlight for this season went to his Bash Brother, Canseco, who became the first player in major-league history to hit 40 homers (ending up with 42) and steal 40 bases in the same season en route to winning the Most Valuable Player award.

"What impressed me was his worth ethic," McGwire said of Canseco. "He has great ability, but you often see players with ability who don't work hard enough to realize their potential. Jose has worked at his game, and he cranked it up to another level this year."

Both Canseco and McGwire were ready when the A's opened the American League play-offs against the Red Sox. Canseco again led the way with three homers and McGwire added one as the A's swept Boston four straight to advance to the World Series against the NL champion Los Angeles Dodgers.

That Series will forever be remembered for the home run an injured Kirk Gibson hit off Dennis Eckersley in the opener, which set the stage for the Dodgers' triumph in five games.

While Gibson's homer was a thrilling moment for the Dodgers and their fans, it was a frustrating one for McGwire and the A's, who thought they were going to win the first game. McGwire wasn't surprised, however, that Gibson had done something heroic.

"Gibson is the most intense player I've ever seen," McGwire said in a diary he kept for *Inside Sports*. "He'll do anything to win, whether it's hitting a home run or making a diving catch or breaking up a play at second base. When he swings and misses at the plate, you can see the pained expression on his face. That's how much he wants to win. He's certainly an inspiration to the Dodgers, and although I was playing against him, I admire any player who is that competitive."

As McGwire sat in the A's locker room trying to cope with the loss and Gibson's homer, he didn't know that in a couple of days he was going to be the one celebrating the special moment of hitting a game-winning homer in the World Series.

After the Dodgers also won game two, the Series moved back to Oakland and McGwire gave the A's a 2–1 win with his ninth-inning blast off former teammate Jay Howell.

"Jay threw me nothing but fastballs, which surprised me," McGwire said in his diary account. "The Dodgers' book on me was that I was a good curveball hitter, so Jay was determined not to throw one to me. It might have been a little pride on his part, too, because Mets pitcher David Cone had made fun of the fact that Howell had thrown so many curveballs against them in the National League Championship Series.

"Anyway, I got all of the seventh fastball that Howell threw me and hit it on a line to left field. I've hit enough home runs to know what it feels like, so the moment I hit it, I thought, 'That's it, that's a home run.' I just jogged out of the batter's box and threw up my arms in celebration. But then as I watched the ball, it dipped a little, and I thought it might not go out after all, so I started running."

The ball did clear the fence, and about the only time McGwire had to cherish the moment was when he made the jog around the bases.

"I never got a chance to savor it," McGwire said. "As soon as I had 'bashed' my teammates, I was grabbed for TV interviews. I had to be at this station and then that station, and then I had to go upstairs to the media interview room and answer the same questions again for 45 minutes. I never got a moment to think about the thrill of winning a World Series game with a home run.

"That was the first time the circus atmosphere of the Series really struck home for me. Oh, I had certainly noticed all of the media around before and after games. We have a small clubhouse, anyway, and you couldn't walk from one end to the other because of all the writers. I had gotten accustomed to a lot of media attention when I hit 49 homers as a rookie, and that hadn't really bothered me.

"But this did. I really would have liked a chance to go off by myself for just a moment or two and think about what I had done, but I never got that chance."

McGwire had a chance to be a hero again in game four, batting with the bases loaded in the seventh inning, two outs, and the A's trailing 4–3. Howell again was on the mound.

"I swear, Howell threw me the same exact pitch he'd thrown the night before," McGwire said. "This time I popped it up. If I'd hit it just a millimeter better, I could have driven this pitch, too. But, instead of getting the top part of the bat on the ball, I got under it."

The A's trailed the Series three games to one and faced the formidable task of having to battle Orel Hershiser, the hottest pitcher in the game that year, in game five.

"Ballplayers have a description for a pitcher like Hershiser—they say he's the kind of pitcher who can give you a comfortable 0-for-4," McGwire said. "He is always around the plate, so you feel you can get a good swing at his pitches. But the ball is always moving, so you seldom hit it solidly. And every time you make an out, you go back to the dugout thinking you'll get him the next time."

There wasn't a next time after the game was over. The Dodgers' 5–2 victory gave them the World Championship. McGwire's homer in game three turned out to be his only hit of the Series.

"I had an empty feeling, and I know my teammates felt the same way," McGwire said. "On paper there was no question we had the better team, but the Dodgers played better and they deserved to win."

Failing to win the World Series was not McGwire's only disappointment in 1988. He and wife Kathy decided to end their four-year-old marriage. He had to deal with that during the season but was able to keep it private and out of the media.

"Of course it was on my mind a lot," he said after reporting to spring training the following year. "I think I was professional enough to separate it from my playing. I can see if somebody had a job they didn't really like how going through something like that would affect their work. But I love playing ball; that is all I ever wanted to do."

McGwire had been twenty-one when the couple was married in 1984. "We got married too young," he said. "We did not know what love was all about. We were way, way too young."

Their son, Matthew, was only one, but McGwire said staying together simply because of him would have been wrong.

"Most people stay together for the sake of the

children," he said. "But children are smart. They can figure out what's going on. I thought it would be better for him to grow up in two happy households instead of one unhappy one."

McGwire had confided in La Russa while in the midst of his personal troubles and instructed the manager to let him know if he witnessed any change in attitude or thought there was a carryover of McGwire's personal problems into his play on the field.

The divorce was amicable, and McGwire and his ex-wife share custody of son Matthew. She has since remarried; Mark has not.

"I really don't see why people can't come out as friends through the whole thing," McGwire said. "If people become enemies, not only does it hurt you mentally, but it hurts your kids in the long run.

"I have an absolutely wonderful relationship with my ex-wife and a marvelous relationship with her husband. But the bottom line is, when you go through a divorce, it's the children who suffer.

"It's tough for Matthew, but it's not like we sprang this on him. It's the only way of life he's known. At his home, I play golf with his stepfather, watch TV with his family, go to dinner. The relationship couldn't be any better."

McGwire was ready to concentrate exclusively on baseball as the 1989 season began. He did not get as involved in off-season activities as he had a year earlier, although he did win the AT&T Pebble Beach National Pro-Am Celebrity Challenge golf tournament, beating actor Chris Lemmon, the son of Jack Lemmon.

McGwire arrived in Arizona early, unlike Canseco, who had spent the winter very much in the news after being ticketed for driving 125 mph in Miami and committing other traffic violations in Phoenix.

McGwire, who often said he probably would have become a police officer had he not been successful in baseball, did not condone Canseco's actions but noted the story received more attention than it would have if Canseco had not been involved.

"It's like nobody in this world has made a mistake," McGwire said. "Nobody else has gotten a ticket for speeding. Why make such a big deal of it? He's another person, but just because he's Jose Canseco, it's worldwide news.

"That really upsets me. If it's Joe Blow speeding, big deal. Nobody knows about it. But if it's Jose Canseco, it goes nationwide on the news. Heck, we're human. He's only 24 years old. How many people who are 24 years old live their life perfectly?"

The response to McGwire's argument is that by becoming a professional athlete that person accepts a little bit of responsibility and the realization that if he or she does make a mistake that involves breaking the law, the chances are pretty good the story will wind up in the newspaper. Athletes who don't accept that they will lose some of the privacy and a "normal" citizen's anonymity are mistaken.

McGwire wasn't there when Canseco was stopped for speeding or one of his other violations, so he didn't know the circumstances and whether any innocent people were at risk. It's surprising he took the stance he did because of his interest in law enforcement and other comments he has made over the years about wishing he had the power to arrest someone.

"You know when you're driving down the street and you see maniacs driving around," he said in a 1987 interview, "I'd just like to have that power, driving that squad car or wearing that uniform, to stop those people from doing wrong things. There are times when I'm in a car and I wish I could pull a guy over and give him a ticket or throw him in the squad car and bring him down to the station."

McGwire said he thought he would like the variety of police work, that it would not be the kind of job where he would be doing the same routine work day after day but a job filled with excitement, much like being a baseball player.

One time when he was accompanying officers on their rounds, he put on a bullet-proof vest and followed officers, with their guns drawn, into a house for a drug bust. The officers kicked down the door and shot a pit bull. The dealer was arrested but only had a few bags of marijuana in his possession.

"It wasn't as big as they thought it was going to be," McGwire said. "Policemen tell me that going on a drug bust has the same exhilaration as hitting a home run."

Canseco, as it turned out, didn't figure much in the A's plans at the start of the 1989 season. He broke a bone in his left wrist during spring training and missed the first half of the year.

McGwire, after starting the season on a most promising note by hitting eight homers in spring training, hit one that counted on opening day as the A's beat Seattle 3–2. Only a week later, however, his season took a downturn when he was placed on the disabled list for the first time in his career.

The injury was originally diagnosed as a herniated disk in his back, but then doctors determined it wasn't that serious and basically was a flare-up of previous back problems and one that would continue to cause him occasional trouble throughout his career. He was told to begin a specific routine of exercises, which McGwire did.

Being inactive for the first time in his career, however, was hard for McGwire. He tried to stay busy by building cabinets in his home and exercising, but he said it would have driven him nuts to just sit around his house all day. He found that A's fans also were eager for him to get back in the lineup.

"I went to the post office late at night to turn in my taxes," he said. "I went with a scraggly beard and glasses because I didn't think I'd get noticed. Some guy comes up and says, 'I hope your back's better.'"

McGwire missed 14 games and returned to the lineup on April 26. The following day, he hit two homers in a 9–4 win over the Orioles. He had another homer to celebrate a week later when he finally connected off his old nemesis, Tom Henke, for a game-winning grand slam with two outs in the ninth, turning a would-be 5–4 loss to Toronto into an 8–5 victory.

"I think every pitcher knows when they own you," McGwire said. "I'm going up in that situation knowing I've struck out every time against him. I'm looking for anything to hit. Fortunately, I got a fast-ball I could handle and I hit it out of the ballpark."

McGwire hit his 100th career homer on July 5, off Kansas City's Charlie Leibrandt. It came in the 1,400th at-bat of his career, the second-fastest in major-league history. Only Hall of Famer Ralph Kiner reached 100 homers faster, doing it in 1,351 at-bats.

McGwire took that news in stride but was more upset that he wasn't able to retrieve the ball as a me-mento. The woman who caught the ball demanded cash in exchange, and when the A's countered with an offer of another ball and a bat, they got no re-sponse.

What McGwire didn't like about the homer was that it again made him the center of attention, a posi-tion he doesn't like.

"I think he likes the limelight, I just don't think he likes talking about himself," La Russa said. "I think he likes the limelight of going to bat in the ninth inning with the game on the line."

The absence of Canseco put more attention on McGwire. If he didn't hit a home run or at least get a hit, the media usually pointed it out, a fact that both-ered McGwire, especially considering the other good veteran hitters in the A's lineup.

"Mark McGwire is a bona fide, legitimate fran-chise-type player," La Russa said. "But there isn't a franchise player who exists that carries a club by himself. That's a misconception."

There was no mistaking how many people were fans of McGwire, many of them children. He had a special moment in July when he got to meet one of his fans, a six-year-old boy named Travis who suffered from cerebral palsy.

McGwire had been Travis's idol ever since the little boy was able to follow baseball on television, and he hugged the boy and gave him an A's cap and a baseball autographed: "To Travis, my buddy."

Moments like that were special for McGwire, who had almost an exact repeat of his 1988 season. He hit 33 homers, one more than in 1988, and drove in 95 runs, four less than in 1988, but saw his batting average drop again, this time down to .231. Becoming only the second player (Canseco was the first) to hit 30 or more homers each of his first three years in the major leagues wasn't much of a consolation for McGwire when he looked at his batting average.

"I get upset because I'm not a .230 hitter," McGwire said. "I'm leaving men in scoring position, and I'm paid to drive in runs. If it were anybody else they might not notice, but if you're a Mark McGwire, a Jose Canseco, a Joe Carter, people expect a lot out of you, maybe too much."

Again, the subject of how well he had done as a rookie reared its ugly head.

"Sometimes I sit back and say, 'Why couldn't I have a normal rookie year?'" McGwire said, but he then adds, "I'd never ever give up what I did."

All of the slumps and misguided suggestions and criticisms made McGwire grow up, giving him an education in life.

"I've really grown as a person," McGwire said. "I've seen how people treat you in certain situations. After the 1987 season, I thought I'd really let a lot of people take advantage of me, of my time. So in 1988 I tried to budget my time and people got upset. People started assuming I'd changed into a bad guy. Hey, I was just trying to be who I am. I'm the same person."

One of the people who tried to counsel McGwire was his former teammate Reggie Jackson. Nobody can really tell you how to get out of a slump, Jackson said; it's something every player goes through and has to deal with by himself.

"You get down," Jackson said. "And everybody tells you to think positive and that kind of stuff. It's wonderful to think positive . . . until you get to the plate and go 0-for-15. Then the positive stuff is over."

McGwire did have one positive note to concentrate on—the team was playing well and winning again, headed toward its second consecutive division title and another shot in the league play-offs, this time against Toronto.

A trade with the Yankees in June had brought Rickey Henderson back to Oakland, and he had provided a big spark to the club, especially when McGwire and Canseco were not hitting.

"People look at us and think we're a power team, but we do a lot of other things as well," McGwire said. "We steal bases, move guys over, take guys out at second base. You don't win 99 games hitting home runs every game."

Henderson was a big part of that, McGwire said.

"He's taken a lot of pressure off all of us," McGwire said. "The attention is spread throughout the ball club."

Manager Tony La Russa thought McGwire and Canseco would emerge from the season as better players in the future.

"Jose and Mark went through a lot this season, but I think it's made them both better players and teammates," La Russa said. "Jose had to deal with the injury and then took a lot of heat because of all the problems with the police and his cars. But he was able to focus on the job at hand. He's a professional.

"Mark struggled at the plate, but still did enough to get his homers and RBIs. It's a credit to both of them that we're back in the play-offs. We wouldn't be here without them."

La Russa tried to take some of the pressure off McGwire by often dropping him as low as sixth or seventh in the batting order. He tried to develop patience, not swinging at bad pitches, and taking walks if the pitchers were giving them to him. Almost amazingly, he was productive almost every time he did get a hit—his 95 RBIs came on just 113 hits.

The A's clicked in the play-offs, behind the lead of Henderson, and beat the Blue Jays four games to one. McGwire had a good series, hitting .389 with his third career postseason homer. Waiting to meet the A's in the World Series were their Bay Area brothers, the Giants, and waiting for McGwire was his former Olympic teammate Will Clark.

The comparison between McGwire and Clark was inevitable. Clark had enjoyed a banner year in 1989. The Giants could have drafted McGwire ahead of Oakland but didn't and a year later took Clark in the first round out of Mississippi State. Clark was the key player on the Giants, who were making their first World Series appearance since 1962.

McGwire was happy for Clark and his success but said he didn't think any head-to-head comparison was valid because they were two different kinds of players, even though both played first base.

"That doesn't mean I can't help win a game for this team," McGwire said. "I knew right away that Will was going to be a star. This season he had has not surprised me one bit. He's simply a great player, and he'll have more seasons like the one he had this year."

McGwire said he was going into the World Series focusing not on Clark but simply on winning, something the A's didn't do the previous year. "I'll do what I'm capable of doing," he said. "But if I don't get a hit and we win, I'll be happy. If I hit .500 and we lose, I'll be unhappy."

McGwire didn't go hitless, getting three hits in the opener and one in game two as the A's won the first two games in Oakland. The Series shifted to San Francisco for game three on October 17, and McGwire and the rest of the players were finishing their preparations for the game when an earthquake struck, shaking Candlestick Park.

Having lived in California his entire life, Mc-Gwire had experienced many earthquakes but none quite at a moment like this. The worst damage was away from the ballpark, and luckily nobody at the ballpark was seriously injured or killed.

Since the entire Bay Area was affected, however, baseball officials postponed the continuation of the series until the area had made somewhat of a recovery. The A's headed to Phoenix to work out for a couple of days at their spring training facility, trying to stay sharp and focused.

Fans paying to attend the A's workouts raised more than $40,000 for the victims of the earthquake.

The Series resumed on October 27, and the A's bombed the Giants 13–7 to take a commanding three games to none lead. Oakland was only ahead 4–3 in the fourth when McGwire made his biggest contribution of the night, a diving stop that ended the inning and prevented the tying run from scoring. The A's completed the four-game sweep the following day with a 9–6 win, making them the World Champions.

McGwire still believes the victory was spoiled because of the earthquake. That is all anybody remembers about the Series, not giving the A's credit for their victory.

"We had to respect the people who died," Mc-Gwire said. "We had to respect what happened in Northern California. We didn't get to celebrate. No champagne. No parade. We had a rally. There'll always be an asterisk next to our '89 championship."

Almost ironically, McGwire was the only Oakland regular who did not hit a home run during the Series.

As much for his career success as for what he did in 1989, the A's nearly tripled McGwire's salary for the 1990 season, signing him to a one-year contract worth $1.5 million.

The signing came one day before McGwire and the A's were scheduled for an arbitration hearing, which almost always produces bitter feelings between the two sides.

"Intelligent clubs realize the arbitration process is detrimental with a player with whom they want a long-term relationship," said Bob Cohen, McGwire's agent. "Certainly, the A's fit into that category.

"No one likes to hear an employer say, 'He's good, but he doesn't do that well.' It's not a love-in. It's a finger-pointing situation, and players don't walk away from those things having great positive feelings for the club."

There wasn't much love between any of the players and owners as the spring training camps prepared to open in 1990. The owners decided to lock the players out of camp in hopes of reaching a new labor agreement and ending the threat of another players' strike during the season.

McGwire always was of the opinion that spring training was too long, so he didn't really mind the extra delay in reporting to Arizona, but it forced him to find other things to do with his time.

On one day, he accompanied two friends who were Alameda, California, police officers on their rounds. "These guys have watched me work; now I get to watch them work," McGwire said.

McGwire said he particularly enjoyed standing close enough to listen to the conversations between the officers and motorists who had just been stopped for speeding.

"I like to listen to what the people say," he said. "I hear excuses people give when they ask for an autograph. It's great to hear excuses here."

As the players finally reported to spring training, McGwire was hoping that he wouldn't have to make excuses for another subpar year, or that other people wouldn't be making excuses for him.

Mentally, he was more focused on not repeating the mistakes he had made the previous two years, and he also thought it might be nice if he caught a break once in a while.

"I've never played a full season at any level and not hit for a good average before last year," McGwire said. "When the hits weren't coming, I'd try to brew something up. I started really pressing, and things just got worse.

"I was hitting bullets everywhere, and they were being caught. There are no excuses, but that's the way it was. Every day I'd feel great, but every night it would be 0-for-4 or 0-for-3. The greatest frustration for a hitter is to hit the ball well and have nothing to show for it."

Hitting coach Merv Rettenmund agreed with McGwire about the bad luck he seemingly endured all season.

"I've been in baseball 20 years and Mark hit the hardest .231 I've ever seen," Rettenmund said. "For a while after the break he was hitting the ball harder than anybody in the league, and his average kept going down. It had to be tough on him."

Trying to make every at-bat be the one that reversed his string of misfortune, McGwire began making too many adjustments and fell into the rut of bad habits, which only make getting out of a prolonged slump that much harder.

"You could see it in his swing," La Russa said. "He got off his normal stroke and started trying to overpower the ball, to pull everything, and that's not his normal stroke."

Karl Kuehl, the player development director who had worked extensively with McGwire when he was in the minors, also spent time trying to see if he could help figure out what was going wrong.

"Mark always was the kind of guy who didn't want to take instruction," Kuehl said. "He had had success and he didn't want to mess with it. Mark would not look at a video when he had done something wrong. He only wanted to look at the at-bats where he had done well.

"I learned something from that. When you're trying to offer instruction, too often you tell a player what he is doing wrong. In Mark's case, the only approach that worked was building on what he was doing well. It was a positive approach, and I believe in that.

"So often in baseball the way we teach is: 'Look

at this. Now we've got to fix this.' Mark didn't want to hear that or look at it."

Despite all of the positive reinforcement from Kuehl, La Russa, and others, 1990 was an all-too-familiar year for McGwire. He got his homers again—becoming the first player in major-league history to hit 30 or more homers in each of his first four seasons—but his average stayed in the .230s.

His 30th homer, on August 15, was a memorable one—a grand slam off Boston's Rob Murphy in the 10th inning that gave the A's a 6–2 victory. The blast slammed off a beer advertisement at the Oakland Coliseum 50 feet above the playing field and 400 feet from home plate.

A boy retrieved the ball, and his father called the A's later and offered to trade it for play-off tickets. The A's declined but did offer two balls autographed by McGwire, and the father accepted.

Special moments like that, however, were too few and far between for McGwire.

He still was hitting homers and driving in runs, yet Rettenmund said the only question people kept asking was, "What's wrong with Mark McGwire?" Every so-called expert had his own theory about why McGwire's average had dropped from .289 his rookie year in 1987 into the .230s, while his homer and RBI numbers had remained relatively constant.

Some people blamed it on his divorce. Others said he was being victimized by his home park, the Oakland Coliseum; still others said he had lost his aggressiveness and was walking too often. There was a theory that he had developed a loop in his swing, and another was that his poor vision wasn't being adequately corrected and he was having trouble seeing the ball.

"I get real irritated, sure," McGwire said in early September. "The point is that I have so many at-bats now it's almost impossible to make my average respectable. I'm so far in the hole that I'd have to hit 1.000 [for the rest of the season] to get to .250.

"I'm just trying to stay positive and take it a day at a time, to contribute the best I can. I'm tired of talking about it and analyzing it. I'll start from scatch when the season's over. In the meantime I obviously feel I'm doing something right. There's a smile on my face and I'm in the lineup every day.

"It's probably the weirdest year I've had in organized ball. You try to pinpoint a spot to correct it. It's not because of lack of work. I work too hard. I just don't know what it is."

McGwire had to look for the positive numbers, like his season totals of 39 homers and 108 RBIs, both the best since his rookie year, and ignore the negative, like the .235 average. It helped that the A's again won the AL West for the third consecutive year, giving fans and the media another subject to focus on, as the team prepared to face Boston for the AL pennant.

One thing McGwire would not let himself do was be drawn into comparisions linking him and Canseco, who hit .274 but finished behind McGwire in homers (with 37) and RBIs (with 101).

"Jose is the best player in the game, by far," Mc-Gwire said. "I'm not comparable to him. I never set expectations to be a superstar or to be a Hall of Famer. All I want to do is play this game."

McGwire did admit that he tried to learn from Canseco, not so much about baseball but about his easygoing manner and how he never seemed to let anything bother him, whether it was a baseball problem or a problem off the field.

"Nothing bothers Jose," McGwire said. "Not one bad at-bat or one game or a week or all that stuff off the field. He goes on like it never happened. I can put things away, but at times, things bother me. I sit in the dugout and watch Jose. I can't say he amazes me, because nothing he does amazes me anymore. There's no one like Jose. I can't do what he does, but he can do what I do."

Both McGwire and Canseco wanted to help the A's beat the Red Sox and get back to the World Series for the third consecutive year. Oakland did get there, with a four-game sweep of Boston, but it had little to do with any positive contributions from either of the A's big sluggers. McGwire hit .182 for the four games and Canseco .154.

Not only was success becoming a pattern for the A's players; it was becoming something the fans expected as well, and that sometimes caused problems, Weiss said.

"There were fans who wouldn't buy play-off tickets because they said they were waiting for the World Series," Weiss said.

McGwire had played in the majors for four seasons and was playing in his third World Series. Some of the greatest players in the history of the game, like Ernie Banks, never made it to the Fall Classic once.

"When you are a young player you don't really understand it," McGwire said. "You are caught up in such a short time in your career. Later in your career you get wiser and you appreciate the game and how difficult it is to win. When you are younger you just go with the flow."

The repeated success might have made the A's a little overconfident heading into the Series against Cincinnati, but the Reds quickly got their attention when Jose Rijo shut them out in the opener and they pounded Dave Stewart for a 7–0 victory. Talk that the Series would be a runaway was over, yet that's exactly what it turned out to be—a sweep by the Reds.

In three seasons, the A's had won a total of 306 games but had only one World Championship flag flying above the Oakland Coliseum. McGwire and the rest of the A's went home for the winter disappointed, and McGwire was hoping that maybe in 1991 he would be able to find the cure for his ailing batting average.

He didn't know the problem was only going to get worse.

HITTING BOTTOM

The only good piece of news McGwire received after the 1990 season was that he had accomplished one of his career goals—coaches and managers in the American League had voted him the Gold Glove first baseman.

"I was really happy when I found out," McGwire said. "It's quite an honor and I'm not going to kick back now and relax—there's too many good first basemen out there. I'd just like to show it can happen again, that it wasn't a fluke.

"I've always been a hard worker at defense. You know you are going to have days at the plate, but you can make people overlook those bad days with good defense. You know, kill a rally with a spectacular stop down the line, make a tough play in a key situation.

I've always said you can win as many games with your glove as you can with your bat."

Despite his low batting average, La Russa and the A's continued to stick McGwire in the lineup every day, because he was able to separate defense from offense and never carried a bad at-bat with him into the field.

He didn't make his first error of the year until July 25. That halted a two-year streak of 103 consecutive errorless games, and he finished the season commiting only five errors in 1,429 chances, as he broke Don Mattingly's five-year hold on the Gold Glove.

"To me it's the biggest individual achievement I ever got," McGwire said. "It means a lot to me that people know you can play defense as well as being a good offensive player."

McGwire also earned recognition for being one of the few Oakland players willing to speak up after the World Series loss to the Reds and listen to the criticism directed toward the team.

"Sometimes you want to put a towel around your face and hope no one will recognize you, but you can't give excuses," McGwire said. "I hate excuses. You have to tell what really happened—they kicked our butt.

"I think everyone knows we didn't do anything. We played exactly like we did in 1988 and the same thing happened. But look what we did in 1989—we came back just as strong and won it, something I think can happen again this year."

Just as he didn't want to offer or hear any ex-

cuses about the A's disappointing performance, Mc-
Gwire was fed up with excuses for his low batting
average. He wanted people to start concentrating
more often on what he was doing well: hitting more
homers than anyone else in baseball during his four
years in the majors.

But some people were suggesting—bringing
back comparisons that had been made when Mc-
Gwire first went to USC—that he was turning into
Dave Kingman.

Kingman hit 442 homers in his career with a
.236 average. Harmon Killebrew took his 573 homers
and .256 average to the Hall of Fame. Thanks in good
measure to his .289 rookie average, McGwire's career
average after 1990 stood at .253.

"I just want to be recognized as one of the best,"
McGwire said. "The last two years I didn't think I was
the hitter I really am. It just wasn't there. When
you're not doing the things you're capable of doing,
you're not getting hits and you're not driving in runs.

"It's funny; I read in one of the papers that my
average dropped and it actually went up from the
year before. But when you're down in that .230 range,
people are going to look at that; I understand that.
Hitting .230—it's not acceptable in my mind either."

The A's made a couple of off-season moves they
hoped would produce positive results for McGwire.
Rick Burleson was hired as the new hitting coach,
and McGwire's old pal Reggie Jackson rejoined the
team as a coach.

McGwire himself gave indications he was going

to be more willing to listen to suggestions than he had been in the past, admitting that part of the problem was likely his own hardheadedness.

"I thought it was just going to happen instead of working on it," he said. "I've hit for average ever since I was a little kid. Then I didn't, and I had to check myself."

Said Jackson, "He's gotten home run–conscious. He's forgotten about hitting the ball away from him. And the reason he's been able to do that is because he has tremendous success hitting the ball out of the ballpark. He's not covering the outside part of the plate."

McGwire and his agent, Bob Cohen, were able to work out a new one-year contract that gave McGwire more than a $1 million raise from 1990, again without going through the bitter arbitration process. The A's would have had to go on the attack against McGwire's low batting average just at the same time they were trying to motivate him to forget about the past three seasons and concentrate on 1991.

McGwire did forget about the past in 1991, but only because those bitter memories were replaced by an even more dreadful season.

When McGwire thought matters couldn't possibly get any worse, they did. He hit a career-low .201 and might have fallen below .200 had he not been held out of the lineup at the end of the season. The only parts of his offensive game that had been positive, homers and RBIs, dropped as well. His string of 30-plus homer seasons ended as he hit 22, and his RBI total fell from 108 to 75.

Mark McGwire, as an Oakland Athletics rookie in 1987.
(UPI/Corbis-Bettmann)

McGwire takes great pride in his fielding and has been a Gold Glove winner. Here he is as an A's rookie at first base. (UPI/Corbis-Bettmann)

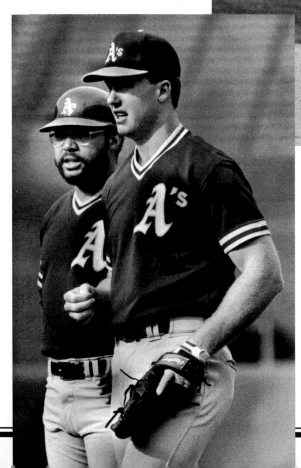

Reggie Jackson was an important early mentor to McGwire. (UPI/Corbis-Bettmann)

Rookie year, home run number 49, off the Cleveland Indians'
John Farrell, on September 29, 1987. (UPI/Corbis-Bettmann)

1988 American League Championship Series: McGwire homers
against Boston in game three. (UPI/Corbis-Bettmann)

The "Bash Brothers," McGwire and Jose Canseco.
(UPI/Corbis-Bettmann)

Two scenes from 1989:
McGwire sliding in safe at
home against Cleveland
(catcher Joel Skinner
leaps for a high throw),
and "bashing" teammate
Dave Henderson after
Henderson's home run
against Toronto.
(Both UPI/Corbis-Bettmann)

He can't hit home runs every at bat: A broken bat single in the fifth inning of the 1989 World Series opener against the San Francisco Giants. (UPI/Corbis-Bettmann)

McGwire and comedian Bill Murray talk hitting during the 1990 All-Star Game workout at Wrigley Field in Chicago. (UPI/Corbis-Bettmann)

Meet me in St. Louis: McGwire fell in love with the city and its fans after he joined the team following the trade from Oakland. (Agence France Presse/ Corbis-Bettmann)

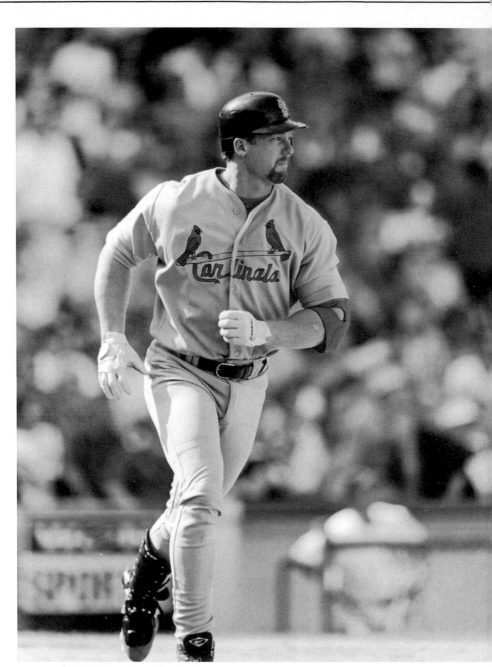

McGwire signed a long-term contract to stay in St. Louis and instantly became one of the city's most popular athletes. (Agence France Presse/Corbis-Bettmann)

His average was not above .219 after June 1, and it bottomed out below .200 for a three-week stretch, reaching a low mark of .187 on July 26.

McGwire's past success still made him popular with All-Star voters, and he was elected the starting first baseman for the game in Toronto. In a further testimony to an awful season, however, McGwire couldn't attend the game because of a burst eardrum, which made it impossible for him to fly.

McGwire's name came up in trade rumors for the first time in his career, with the A's reportedly discussing a deal with the Angels that would have sent McGwire to California and brought Wally Joyner to Oakland. The Angels declined for a couple of reasons, worrying about what had happened to McGwire's skills and concerned that he might leave as a free agent after the 1992 season.

The A's promoted a first baseman from Triple A in late August, Ron Witmeyer, and La Russa had to go to great lengths to assure the media that it wasn't a threat to McGwire's status as the starting first baseman.

"This is not a change of guard at first base," La Russa said. "We had a chance to bring up a position player and he [Witmeyer] was having a solid year. So he deserves the promotion. And I'll see what playing time I can generate for him. That's all it is."

La Russa was asked why he wouldn't think of platooning McGwire with Witmeyer.

"Because I believe in him, that's why," La Russa said of McGwire.

Even though he still had the support of his manager, McGwirc, for the first time since his rookie year, didn't have the team success to fall back on when he wasn't pleased with his personal success. The A's nose-dived to fourth place, finishing 11 games behind the Twins.

Reporters covering the A's said that by the end of the year McGwire and Burleson weren't even talking. There were some suggestions that Burleson's honesty had hurt McGwire's feelings. Burleson, at La Russa's urging, kept trying to change McGwire's hitting style. Nothing was working, and McGwire admitted he often walked to the plate so confused he had no chance of getting a hit.

"I know there is a tendency to blame Rick," La Russa said in 1992. "But I accept as much blame as anybody about telling Mark things like, 'You're a high-average hitter.' I was the one who was agitating him about 'throwing some base hits in there when you're hitting all those home runs.'

"Rick represented me, and I asked him to do things with McGwire. The story that Burleson took something away from McGwire has always been overplayed. It wasn't that way at all. McGwire's average had been coming down long before then."

For the first time in his life, McGwire disliked baseball. He didn't want to go to the park; he didn't want to face the reporters; he didn't want to think about what was happening.

Children who played on a playground at a school near McGwire's home actually began jeering him instead of cheering, yelling "you stink" when they recognized him. He was so upset he couldn't even laugh.

"It was frustrating trying to climb out of a hole that got deeper and deeper," he reflected later. "It was frustrating listening to all of the hooting and the hollering. I started joking in the clubhouse that I was going to give up baseball to shoot pool for a living or maybe, like some of my friends, become a policeman. I was joking, but there was an element of truth in what I was saying."

His friends and teammates felt for McGwire, but other than being there and continuing to offer support, there wasn't really anything anybody could say or do.

"He was going through hell, but he didn't wear it on his sleeve," Dennis Eckersley told *Sports Illustrated*. "All in all, he handled himself pretty well. In fact, he should be damn proud of the way he acted."

One friend who tried to offer assistance was golfer Billy Andrade, a member of the PGA Tour. He and McGwire became friends after playing together at the AT&T Pebble Beach National Pro-Am in 1990. Andrade invited McGwire to come stay with him during the Las Vegas Invitational in October, a trip McGwire hadn't been able to make for three years, while playing in the World Series.

Andrade and McGwire had just finished a workout when McGwire noticed a television in the corner was on, carrying the World Series game between the Twins and the Braves.

"I could see that it was getting to him," Andrade

told *Sports Illustrated.* "He didn't come right out and say it, but I know what he was thinking: I don't want to be sitting here in a hot tub in Caesar's Palace with Billy. I want to be playing in the Series."

The trip to Las Vegas coincided with a personal journey McGwire took after the 1991 season. He packed his personal belongings in his car after the final game of the year for the drive back to his home near Los Angeles.

He didn't plan on using that five-and-a-half-hour drive as a trip through his soul, but that's what happened. He never turned on the radio or tape player during the entire trip but spent the whole time talking to himself, trying to figure out what he needed to do to straighten out his career and his life.

After divorcing Kathy, he had been seeing another woman, but that relationship had ended in September. His life and his career were in shambles.

"I shouldn't have let that bother me," McGwire said. "I should have been able to separate that part of my life from what was happening on the field, but I couldn't always do that."

McGwire knew it was time to do something. When he got out of the car in Los Angeles, McGwire had made up his mind that he needed help, that he had to see a therapist.

"I had to face the music," McGwire said. "It was the turning point in my life and it just happened to be the turning point in my career, too. No matter who you are in this world, sometimes you have to get slapped in the face. Something has to happen to make you wake up.

"It would have been easy for me to hide and put my head in a hole and sit down and sulk and say, 'Poor me.' But I didn't have time to do that. I wanted to turn my life around."

Andrade could tell that McGwire's life was about to change when they were together for that week in Las Vegas.

"When we went to the World Series three years in a row and people asked me, 'How does it feel, Mark, to be in the Series?' I put them off," McGwire said. "I thought it would never really sink in until I retired. But right there in Las Vegas, I realized what it meant to play in the Series. I also realized that unless I did something about it, I might never get another chance. So right then and there, I rededicated myself to baseball."

McGwire hit the weight room with that new desire. His younger brother J. J., a weight trainer, began working with him and challenged his older brother to get stronger.

"I got all over him one day and told him he was real skinny," J. J. McGwire said. "He saw me growing. I guess I motivated him."

The workouts helped McGwire add 20 pounds of muscle and physically made him feel better about himself.

McGwire also began daily eye exercises suggested by Bill Puett, a sports training specialist in San Diego.

"I never knew this, but there are muscles in the eyes that we don't use to their full capacity, and now

I'm just exercising them," McGwire said. Puett said the exercises were designed to improve McGwire's reaction time and quickness.

Now it was time to work on his mind. McGwire began to see the therapist and got more involved in those sessions than he intended.

"The counseling started out as a personal thing, but before long it was everything," McGwire said. "Personal, professional, dealing with the media, dealing with fans, dealing with life. I got my mind straight, and everything followed."

McGwire said it was the first time in his life he learned how powerful his mind could be, that it controlled everything else in his life.

"There are a lot of ballplayers playing this game on strict ability," he said. "They don't use their minds. It's amazing to think I played this game for five years without using my mind.

"It was horrible, and yet it was the biggest learning experience of my life. I learned that I had to be who I am, not somebody who somebody else wants me to be."

The counseling sessions benefited McGwire's mind, and he's not afraid to say it.

"People have this thing called pride, and sometimes they think they don't want to tell people and that if you go to therapy people will think you're crazy," McGwire said. "The people who don't think they have any problems have problems. Everybody has things they can work on and improve on. There's nobody who is perfect in this world."

The A's hired a new hitting coach for the 1992 season, former Angels manager Doug Rader, and team executives thought maybe if McGwire got a head start on the season, it would help produce positive results.

Karl Kuehl brought in McGwire's old coach Ron Vaughn, and McGwire came to Arizona for a week in January, passing up the Pebble Beach golf tournament.

"We just worked and went through all of the drills we used to do," Kuehl said. "Mark was coming off those bad years, and he was struggling to find himself. It was important to him.

"The basic swing was there. The biggest difference was what he did with his hands, and he just made up his mind that he was going to get his hands inside the ball."

Changing that helped shorten his swing, which brought the bat through the zone quicker and in the drills immediately began producing better results.

After a few days, McGwire, Vaughn, and Kuehl were joined by Rader.

"I thought it would give Doug and Mac a chance to get to know each other without a lot of other players around," Kuehl said. "Mac and Rader really hit it off, and that was a big thing for him. If nothing else, he saw that we really believed in him and knew that he could do it.

"He was getting to know himself and hitting pretty well by then. Mac has always been a pretty basic hitter. He was the kind of guy that if he had to think about something, he wasn't going to hit."

Rader's philosophy mirrored that approach. He kept hitting simple—see the ball and hit the ball—and didn't try to overload McGwire's mind with too many suggestions and changes.

"A lot of it is very subtle," Rader said at the time. "I'm reluctant to talk for the reason nothing should be directed to me in the way of credit and because any kind of instruction would be confidential."

McGwire later said that when Rader addressed the team's hitters at the opening of spring training, he asked a question: "What is the object of being a hitter?"

"There was silence; then finally someone said, 'To get a hit?'" McGwire said. "And Doug said, 'Correct.'"

McGwire's respect for Rader is what enabled the relationship to work.

"He's what I need," McGwire said. "He'll sit there and be very, very positive and not tell me to change things. The times we've had talks, he makes so much sense. Basically, I'm doing what I'm capable of doing instead of what people want me to do. It's a tough thing to do, and I learned the hard way."

McGwire also learned the truth about the Gold Glove award when he didn't repeat as the first baseman on the AL squad despite actually making one less error than he had when he won the award in 1990. Mattingly regained possession of the statue, despite playing only 127 games at first.

"I'm totally convinced the Gold Glove means offense and has nothing to do with defense," McGwire said. "I even had people tell me I had a better year defensively last year than the year before, when I won it. It upset me I didn't get recognized."

There was one more piece of unfinished business for McGwire to complete before he was ready to move forward into 1992. He had to sign a contract, and in a rare gesture in baseball these days, he didn't seek a raise.

"I had a year where I didn't do what I'm capable of doing, and I didn't deserve a raise," McGwire said. "I have to feel good about what I do, and I did feel good about that. I don't want money to get in the way of what I'm doing, which is playing baseball. I'm not a guy who says, 'I've got to beat this guy and get paid more.' People lose what it's about. It's a game, a kid's game. So much is made of money.

"You hear so much about money and the expectations that go with money. Sure, if you make millions and millions, people are going to expect a lot out of you, because if you're getting paid that much, you've got to do what you're paid for."

McGwire and his agent instructed the Players Association to file his arbitration request at the same salary he had made in 1991, only the union forgot to include a $25,000 bonus he had earned for making the All-Star team. His request was filed at $2.85 million, making him the first player to actually file for a pay cut. McGwire didn't find out about the mistake until after the arbitration figures were exchanged, because he was in Australia with Andrade, working as his caddy for a golf tournament.

His agent, Cohen, said, "Mark wasn't looking to make a statement. It says a lot about him. It took guts on his part. I don't care what other agents say or what the Players Association says. I have a client and I have to look after the best interests of my client.

"He [McGwire] said, 'Let's get last year behind us.' It took honesty and it took some guts, but honesty more than anything else."

McGwire ended up signing his fifth consecutive one-year deal, for $2.6 million, taking a cut of $250,000.

"I couldn't look myself in the mirror and say I deserved a raise," McGwire said.

When he did look in the mirror, ready to begin the 1992 season, McGwire finally liked what he saw staring back at him. He was happy again, and that meant there would be a lot of unhappy pitchers in the season to come.

10

REGAINING CONTROL

McGwire's teammates knew they were looking at a changed man when he showed up for spring training. Gone was the clean-shaven, baby-faced McGwire, replaced by a man with a goatee.

"I tried a beard two or three times over the winter," McGwire said. "But some social occasion always came up that made me self-conscious about it. Still, I felt I really needed something, and about three weeks before spring training I started the goatee. I think it has added about five years to my baby face."

The extra pounds of muscle also convinced McGwire's teammates that the long downward cycle had reached its nadir. McGwire was smiling again and laughing. He even took the responsibility of becoming the team's muffin and doughnut supplier, stopping every morning on his way to the A's complex to pick up two boxes of bakery goods.

"Got to keep the guys happy," McGwire said.

Keeping McGwire himself happy was important if the A's wanted to rebound from their disappointing season of 1991.

As that dismal year was about to end, McGwire couldn't help but notice a fan acting strange in the stands at the Oakland Coliseum. Every time McGwire reached the on-deck circle, this fan was on his feet, yelling McGwire's name and waving his hands wildly.

When he thought he had McGwire's attention, the fan kept pointing his fingers inward.

McGwire had no idea what this was supposed to mean, and curiosity finally overtook him. He waved the fan over and asked him what he was trying to say.

"Go back to your pigeon-toe," the fan said.

The fan was referring to the batting stance McGwire had implemented as a rookie but had abandoned. The advice stuck with McGwire all winter as he made his personal transformation. He found himself pulling out a bat and standing in front of a mirror, trying to rediscover his proper stance and swing.

Those sessions, plus the work with Kuehl, Vaughn, and Rader in Arizona in January, had convinced McGwire the fan was right. He also went back to his old bat, a 34 1/2 inch, 33-ounce Adirondack model.

McGwire led the Cactus League in hitting, and a good start to the regular season was all he needed to put the final touches on his comeback, reinforcing the confidence that he felt. In the first seven games of the season, he slammed five homers, including two off Jack McDowell of the White Sox.

McGwire then apologized to reporters for being boring and saying he didn't want to talk about his hitting.

"I've never liked talking about hitting," McGwire said. "I just don't feel like I should. So that's the way I feel about it. I had two hits today. I wish they had helped us win."

The quick start prevented McGwire from doubting himself again, which might have wiped out all of the positive gains he had made over the winter.

"I just feel good about myself physically, mentally, everything," he said. "I'm a lot happier person, playing baseball and off the field. I had time to think about a lot of things. I have a different outlook on life; yes, I do. Am I a lot wiser? Yes, I am."

The other mental change is that McGwire finally decided to stop fighting the label that he was a home run hitter. Despite his struggles, he still had more homers—175—in his five years in the majors than any other player during that time.

"I decided I wouldn't fight it because that is what I am, a home run hitter," he said. "That's me. That's what God put me here to be. Now if I get a hit to right field you can pretty much count on it being an accident."

McGwire hit 10 homers in April, missing the record shared by six players by one, and added eight

more in May. On June 10 in Milwaukee he hit his
22nd homer of the year, tying his total of the previous
year, and it also was the 200th of his career.

The milestone homer came in the 2,852nd at-bat.
Only four players in history had reached 200 homers
in fewer at-bats—Ralph Kiner, Babe Ruth, Harmon
Killebrew, and Eddie Mathews, all Hall of Famers.

McGwire exchanged an autographed bat for the
ball.

"It's nice to be associated with them," McGwire
said of his select company. "A kid growing up, never
really thinking about it, and then your name is mentioned with theirs. . . . When you think about it, it's
an honor."

After watching McGwire up close for the first
two and a half months of the sesaon, Rader knew a
big part of McGwire's success had been achieved by
finally coming to peace with himself and recognizing
that he had a much greater chance of hitting 40 or
more homers than he did of hitting .300.

"Physically he's able to generate a loop in his
swing which aids the ball in the correct trajectory it
takes to get over the wall," Rader said. "And that's
something that's almost God-given. He has the
strength to get away with a loop. The reason most
people can't use a loop in their swing is because
they're either not strong enough to hit home runs
consistently or they're not strong enough to get the
bat head to the contact point often enough."

McGwire's renewed success once again produced comparisons with his teammate Canseco, who

still had more career homers at that point than Mc-
Gwire, 222 to 200.

Canseco said most people didn't believe that neither he nor McGwire got caught up in personal battles with each other, even on a friendly basis.

"It's funny, but there's none whatsoever,"
Canseco said. "And I tell you that truthfully. People
might think, 'Oh yeah, Jose gets pissed off if McGwire
hits a home run.' But I don't feel that. I'm always pulling for Mac and he's always pulling for me."

Knowing how hard McGwire had worked to battle out of his prolonged slump gave Canseco even
more reason to root for his success.

"A lot of people gave up on him," Canseco said.
"I've been through those times and I know exactly
what it feels like. You learn a lot when you go through
that. You learn who your friends really are and who
you can trust. And what happened is he became a better player because of it."

Other teammates also recognized how far Mc-
Gwire had come to battle back to his true ability.

"It's like he's a totally different person," said reliever Dennis Eckersley. "You've got to give him
credit, especially with all the abuse he took. He
seemed to handle it as well as I've seen it handled.

"People don't understand how tough it was on
Mark, how it ate him up inside. He really never let his
emotions show, but you could tell how it was affect-
ing him. Little things can add up on a person, you
know? It's not always just a slump."

Added Rickey Henderson, "I think it made him

grow up. Right from the start of his career he was successful, and he never saw the downside. When it was over with, he learned from it. It made him a better ballplayer than he was in the years he was dominating. He realized that the game doesn't come as easy as he thought it did."

Even ex-teammates, like Yankees pitcher Scott Sanderson, could notice the difference in the way McGwire went about his business.

"So much of this game takes place above the shoulders," Sanderson said. "Last year Mark looked unsure of himself and unsure of his approach as a hitter. This year you don't see any of that. He looks locked in, like he knows what he wants to do. And I'm happy for him because I know him to be a gentle and caring person. He's a great guy."

McGwire wanted to stay focused on his game plan and the success of the team and cut down on what he considered excessive questions from the media. He still tried to be polite and cordial, but he just didn't understand the necessity of listening to the same questions and repeating the same answers night after night.

His "Sorry, I'm busy" attitude might not have been what reporters and broadcasters wanted to hear, but if it was working for McGwire, he was going to stick with it.

Columnist Bruce Jenkins wrote in the *San Francisco Chronicle* on May 20: "This is the smartest thing McGwire has ever done. He was not the greatest interview in the world to begin with. McGwire has always been the type of athlete who distrusts all media, figuring they've never played the game, don't know a thing and couldn't begin to understand what anyone's doing out there. He's been warm and accommodating in the past, but you'd never hear him talking sports in the earnest, deep-down manner he grants to his buddies and teammates."

What has always bothered McGwire about the media is that they are really only reporting on one-half of a person, the person who performs on the field. They can't report on what kind of a person he is off the field, because they don't see that side of him. They see the public McGwire, but they don't see the private side.

"People did a lot of judging of me," McGwire said about 1991, "but that's the way society is. They build you up to be a top-notch player; then you have a bad year and they want to drop you to the bottom.

"There were so many bad things written about me that people thought that way about me. When they saw me, they thought I was a bad baseball player. You think I like walking around in public like that? But I did. I didn't hide.

"Basically, we're two different people. We're like actors out on the field. But you can't form an opinion from the way a person is on the field."

Reporters, as they are prone to do, tried to look for theories for McGwire's sudden rebirth, just as they had sought theories for why he was struggling to hit more than .200 the year before. There were charts listing all of the possible reasons, which ranged from the change in his batting stance, to the goatee, to his status as a potential free agent at the end of the season. None were totally correct.

By the All-Star break, McGwire had 28 homers and was named to the AL squad for the sixth straight season, including his fifth consecutive start. The game was played in San Diego, but before the game came the home run contest during the team's workouts.

McGwire has said he doesn't care much for these kinds of shows, but he put on a display that made him the featured attraction. The contest had several players from each league competing as a team to see who could get the most homers. A player got 10 outs—anything that wasn't a home run was an out.

After a pop-up on his first swing, McGwire proceded to hit eight consecutive pitches for home runs, surprising even himself.

"I looked up, and I had one out and eight homers," McGwire said. "I was just looking for four."

McGwire's show reached the point where Joe Carter came out of the dugout with a cup of water, just to cool off McGwire. "That was the best thing that happened," McGwire said. "You get tired out there."

McGwire finally reached 12 homers before recording his 10th out. Unfortunately, he didn't save any blasts for the game itself.

His regular-season total climbed to 38 by August 21, when McGwire finally was stopped. He strained a muscle in his right rib cage and was forced onto the disabled list for the second time in his career.

At the time McGwire went down, the A's were in first place, enjoying a five-game lead. Despite that position, GM Sandy Alderson made a move at the trading deadline 10 days later that he thought would be better for the future. Alderson traded Canseco, McGwire's Bash Brother, to Texas for Ruben Sierra, Bobby Witt, and Jeff Russell.

The deal surprised McGwire, but he has never been one to get too involved in what he considers other people's business. McGwire had enjoyed his years with Canseco but also had begun to question how much longer the two of them would be together. Eligible himself to become a free agent in another month, he didn't know if he would be returning to Oakland.

McGwire got back in the lineup in time to help the A's celebrate another Western Division title, but not in time to win another home run crown. He finished the year with 42, losing the honor when Texas's Juan Gonzalez hit his 43rd on the final day of the season.

McGwire was proud that he had proven to himself he wasn't washed up, raising his average back to .268 and finishing with 104 RBIs, all major reasons why the A's won 96 games and the division title.

The play-offs against Toronto began on a promising note as McGwire launched a two-run homer on his first at-bat and the A's won 4–3. It was about the only moment he had to celebrate, however, as the Blue Jays came back and won the series in six games.

Following the final game, La Russa shut the doors to the clubhouse and delivered an emotional 15-minute speech, McGwire said.

While not wanting to be specific about what La Russa said, McGwire said, "The speech was unbelievable. There were tears in the clubhouse."

Winning that series and getting back to the World Series would have made McGwire's comeback even more complete, but he had a lot of reasons to be happy as he headed into the winter.

There were also feelings of uneasiness, however, as he entered the period of free agency and didn't know where it would lead him.

Nothing happened for a while, and McGwire and his agent listened to other teams express interest. There was talk that the A's were looking to cut the team's payroll, and if that was the case, McGwire didn't know where he fit into their plans.

Alderson went to the winter meetings in Louisville in early December convinced that other teams were thinking about trying to hold down costs and trying to negotiate carefully with several top-caliber free agents. Then came an unbelievable week when salaries reached levels never before imagined, with Barry Bonds, Greg Maddux, David Cone, Joe Carter, and others reaching new multimillion-dollar deals.

Despite his own personal feelings, Alderson knew that if the A's were going to remain competitive, especially given the cross-bay Giants' signing of Bonds, the team would have to spend more money on players. The GM went home after the meetings and re-signed Steinbach, Sierra, and pitcher Ron Darling. The one missing signature was McGwire's.

McGwire was getting inquiries from other teams.

He went to Atlanta to check out the city. The White Sox were interested, and he said he almost thought he was headed to Boston.

In the final negotiations, however, McGwire stayed in Oakland, getting his Christmas present a day early by signing a five-year, $28 million contract that included a $7 million signing bonus.

"When you get to free agency, you get to shop around," McGwire said. "I didn't want to jump into anything. I wanted to take my time. I wanted to make the right decision. I know I did."

Gone from Oakland's glory days were Dave Stewart, Jose Canseco, Walt Weiss, Mike Moore, and Carney Lansford, either traded away, lost as free agents, or retired. Still, McGwire thought the nucleus of returning players was more than enough to make the A's a contending team for years to come.

There was only one thing he had not counted on happening.

11

INJURIES ARE NO FUN

Mentally relaxed because of the new contract and his spirit renewed by how well he had played in 1992, McGwire prepared for the 1993 season as hard as he had ever worked in the winter.

Uninterrupted work in the weight room again added more muscle. The play-off loss to the Blue Jays had increased his resolve to come back stronger for the new season, and that's what he did.

He even shaved off his goatee after the loss in Toronto, but he decided he liked his looks better with it, so he grew it back.

His teammates didn't have any wisecracks about the goatee as they had a year earlier, but they were able to ridicule McGwire about his golf game. He and his PGA buddy, Billy Andrade, were partners again in the AT&T Pebble Beach National Pro-Am and were in contention for the title through the final round.

McGwire, who said he hadn't played golf for two years, missed a putt on the 18th hole on the final day of the tournament that would have tied him and Andrade with another pair for first place. Instead, they finished second.

"Pros who miss putts like that for $100,000 don't get ragged the way I have been," McGwire said. "It was about a six-footer (it looked shorter on television) and my pro lined me up wrong."

McGwire's last statement was a private joke about a statement made by Andrade, when he was competing in Australia and McGwire was working as his caddy. Andrade had missed a putt of similar length and had blamed McGwire, saying he lined him up wrong.

That McGwire was able to joke and endure the good-natured ribbing of his teammates was a good sign for the A's, who were counting on him to assume a leadership role on the team that had significantly altered its veteran base of the previous years.

That wasn't a role McGwire envisioned for himself. Leading by example, playing hard on the field, and doing whatever it took to win, yes. But he wasn't, and still isn't, the kind of player who is going to stand up and make fiery speeches in the locker room.

"He knew that if he was coming back to Oakland, some responsibility for the team, for carrying the team, would fall to him," said GM Sandy Alderson. "And in a quiet way, I think he has done that."

The A's radio advertising campaign to sell tickets for the season even included a pitch from McGwire. Persons buying a package of tickets for 20 games earned the right to yell, "Hey, McGwire, you're a bum!" If a person bought the 35-game ticket package, it included the right to yell, "Hey, McGwire, is that a goatee or have you been sucking on a muffler?" That question is followed by McGwire laughing.

If someone bought the entire season package, all 81 games, McGwire informs listeners, he will have the additional right to say, "Hey, McGwire, is that your butt or the Goodyear blimp?"

Then McGwire, in a menacing voice, delivers the kicker for the ad: "Should I hear any of this stuff from a non-season ticket holder, I reserve the right to handle the situation as I see fit."

McGwire said he probably would have not worded the commerical the same way, but he had fun doing the spot.

"A few years ago there's probably no way you would've gotten Mac to do that," said teammate Terry Steinbach. "He's definitely more boisterous now, more outgoing."

Like everyone in baseball, McGwire was saddened by the boat accident in Florida during spring training that killed Cleveland pitchers Steve Olin and Tim Crews. When he learned the city of Cleveland was setting up a trust fund for Olin's three children, McGwire quietly sent a check for $25,000, even though he didn't know Olin and had never played with him.

Making a gesture of that magnitude and not seeking publicity for it was not unusual for McGwire, according to the people who have known him well over the years.

Ted Polakowski, in his work for the A's in Arizona, had developed a relationship with Phoenix Children's Hospital in which he routinely took Rookie League players to the hospital to visit patients. When McGwire was in Phoenix in the fall of 1992, Polakowski asked if he would make one of the trips to the hospital and McGwire said yes.

They took a bunch of A's hats and were distributing them to the children, and McGwire ended up spending much of his time with one particular youngster, a boy about three or four years old, who had a terminal illness and was scheduled to undergo surgery the following day.

"I found out later that the boy passed away while in surgery," Polakowski said. "The parents called and talked about how much they appreciated Mark coming and spending that time with him. They said it was all the boy had talked about and said he even had worn the A's hat into surgery."

Polakowski said that when he told McGwire about the boy's death McGwire was visibly upset but also was glad that the boy's last moments had been happy ones.

McGwire's new contract enabled him to donate more to charity, and he pledged $1,000 per home run to two groups, the Bay Area food banks and a drug-alcohol rehabilitation group.

"It's time to help," he said. "These are two good groups."

The 1993 season began on a good note for McGwire, who hit nine homers in the first six weeks. The quick start, following McGwire's big season in 1992, again prompted talk about home run records and projections and again prompted McGwire to try to downplay his own importance as one of the game's best players.

"I never put myself on an extreme level," he said. "I think I'm a pretty good ballplayer. When I think of talent, well, Jose can do a little more than I can do. He can run, steal bases, play the outfield. He's a more complete player than I am.

"I'm just a first baseman. Kirby Puckett, Barry Bonds—those guys are up at a certain level. I love to watch them. I have to acknowledge that those guys are great. I've never been a jealous person. There's always going to be someone who's better than me. He might be 10 years old right now."

On May 3, the A's played in Yankee Stadium and McGwire had a reason to be happy—he hit two homers and made three key defensive plays. As he was running the bases, however, he felt an unusual pain in his ankle.

The orginal diagnosis was a bruised heel. McGwire continued to play for more than a week before the pain finally forced him onto the disabled list.

McGwire didn't know that he would play in only two more games the rest of the year.

The diagnosis was later changed to a torn tendon. He received shots. He had his foot in a cast. He was activated September 3 and made two pinch-hitting apperances, but he knew there still was something wrong.

On September 24, McGwire underwent surgery in Houston, where Dr. Donald Baxter corrected a partial tear of fascia in his left heel and also shaved a small bone spur. (The fascia is a sheath of connective tissue underneath the skin that supports the arch.)

McGwire was glad to finally know what the problem was after spending most of the season hobbling around and watching the A's, who he thought would be competitive, stumble to a 94-loss, last-place finish.

"It was hard for me to sit and watch," McGwire said. "It was especially hard watching the way we played a lot of the time. I tried to keep the clubhouse loose, joking around and getting on the youngsters, but it was a difficult year for everybody, including the fans."

McGwire also was in for a frustrating season in 1994, a bad year for everybody in baseball because of the threat of a players' strike, which hung over everybody's heads until it eventually did materialize. The strike canceled the last seven weeks of the season, the play-offs, and the World Series.

McGwire was full of optimism as he reported to Arizona in February 1994, saying, "I feel as good as I've ever felt."

What McGwire had seen as he watched the A's disappointing performance in 1993 caused him to become a little more vocal, especially when it came to offering suggestions and ideas to younger players. He also tried to work on their attitude, the way some veteran players had done for him when he was a rookie.

"These young kids today are a lot different than when I came up," McGwire said that spring. "They come up thinking they're such hot stuff. I don't know what they teach them in the minor leagues today, but they're different. I jump on them now because I remember if I loafed as a player, I'd have a Don Baylor, Dave Parker, or Reggie Jackson all over my butt."

McGwire said the attitude he saw from young players about defense bothered him. Not many players spent time in practice to make themselves better fielders, the way he had done.

"You have to make the routine play," he said. "So many kids today try to make the great play and don't make the routine plays. Well, if you make the routine play, the great plays just fall into place."

Different kids also were on McGwire's mind. While on a flight from Atlanta to Oakland, he read about the abduction of a girl from Petaluma, California, named Polly Klaas. McGwire's son, Matthew, was now six years old, and the story bothered McGwire and made him think and worry about other missing children. He joined a public awareness campaign about the missing children that included making a donation of $30,000 to four Bay Area missing children's foundations.

On the field, McGwire again was having problems with a sore back. He didn't play in a Cactus League game until March 24. He did appear in Oakland's opening day lineup for the seventh consecutive season but went down again before April was over, this time suffering a stress fracture in that same troublesome left heel.

That injury sidelined him until June, and a month later he hurt his heel again, which put him back on the disabled list for the rest of the season. In a two-year span, McGwire played only 74 of a possible 276 games. At the time of the strike, the A's were in second place, only a game out of first, but still were eight games below .500.

Trying to fill the void left by McGwire were Troy Neel and Mike Aldrete, and both admitted there was no way they could adequately replace McGwire in the lineup.

"Nobody can take the place of Mark," Neel said. "Just his presence in the lineup is a big thing. It's a great opportunity for me to get to play again, but the big thing is winning, and we need McGwire for that. I've got three years in now, and I don't have a [championship] ring. I don't want to be one of those guys who looks back after 20 years and never has played on a winner. McGwire is a big part of that."

Said Aldrete, "I will be the first to admit that I want McGwire back in the lineup. I have been around long enough to know that I want to do the job to the best of my abilities, but the best of my abilities are not the best of Mark McGwire's abilities. My job has always been that if something happens to Mark, to put my finger in the dike and hold it until he gets back. There is no question that when we put our best team on the field, he is at first base."

The knowledge that he wasn't able to contribute and make the A's a better team was a big part of McGwire's frustration.

"I thought it was fixed before," McGwire said of his heel. "I'm sick and tired of being at 50 percent, 60 percent. I want to be well. That's the most irritating thing about this. It comes down to how I feel about my foot and how I feel about my career."

Admitting he was scared to undergo another operation, McGwire decided he had to do so. On August 30, nearly three weeks after the players' strike began, Dr. Baxter this time operated to "release the lateral plantar fascia" in McGwire's left heel. The surgery a year earlier had only shortened the fascia.

The A's were convinced, as was Dr. Baxter, that all of the heel injuries were related.

Removing the entire fascia meant there was no more connective tissue in the heel for McGwire to tear. Doctors said there was a risk in the operation, because what the fascia does is support the arch. The surgery forced McGwire to begin wearing special arch supports in his shoes.

McGwire knew there were skeptics who really didn't believe he was injured as badly as he said he was, because they couldn't see a bone sticking through his skin. The criticism bothered him.

"There is a playing pain and a not-playing pain," he said. "My career is on the line. I'll give back every cent of my salary if I'm not injured. If anybody is going to question my integrity or my wanting to play the game, let him say it to my face."

La Russa was convinced that McGwire would have played had he been able to withstand the pain.

"My impression is that he tried to go out there and play hurt and he felt a different kind of pain," La Russa said. "It wouldn't do any good for him to stand out there like a cigar-store Indian."

Mentally, the injuries were wearing on McGwire.

"The night I broke it again [in Anaheim] I had just got done talking with J. T. Snow, telling him I'm over it," McGwire said. "Not more than 10 minutes later, I bust it again. For this to happen—the third incident in the same foot—it's absolutely killing me."

Ever since he had begun seeing a therapist after the 1991 season, McGwire had developed a philosphy that everything happened for a reason. He knew he would not have enjoyed the great season he had in 1992 if he had not reached rock bottom the year before. He knew these injuries were happening for a reason, but what upset him the most was that he didn't know what it was.

With knowledge gained by time, McGwire now thinks he knows what those injuries and missing almost all of two seasons did for him. The injuries forced him to sit and watch baseball, not play it, an experience he had never had before.

The injuries forced him to develop his mind and study the game. He learned more about pitching and hitting from watching without the pressure of trying to get a hit himself, without worrying so much about what he was doing that he couldn't watch anybody else.

He also learned, in the opinion of his manager, how much he liked the game and wanted to be out on the field playing.

"He started really studying the competition between the hitter and the pitcher and the catcher," La Russa said. "For those of us who saw him as a young player, this move to be smarter is the thing that's most impressive. He's a really tough out, and he's a really good thinker."

While sidelined with those injuries, reflecting on lessons he had learned in therapy sessions, McGwire realized how important his mind was to any success he might have on the field.

"The one thing most people don't realize is that baseball is not physical; it's mental," McGwire said. "Sure, you've got to have the ability, but you can overcome anything with the mind. The mind is so powerful, and I think I'm too strong to let any of that extraneous stuff bother me."

McGwire convinced himself that he was going to get well again, but he didn't know when he would have the chance to play again because he didn't know when the strike was going to end.

When owners began spring training in 1995 with replacement players, McGwire spoke out strongly against the owners, which upset La Russa. McGwire accused the owners of trying to break the union.

"It's going to be a mockery of the game," McGwire said about the plans for replacement players, generally minor leaguers who were not considered top prospects. "As for these scabs, they want to play in the big leagues, but it's sad. They're not going to be playing in the big leagues. It's called scab ball. That's not the big leagues. It's really, really sad."

What also bothered McGwire was the public perception, based on the salaries the players make, that the players were the ones who were ruining the game. He saw the situation differently.

"You have a group of owners that wants to take away every right we've earned," McGwire said. "That's wrong. They want to take everything away. We're not saying we want total control. We're saying that it seems like the owners want total control of everything.

"It's almost like these owners think we don't want to play. Hell no. You think I'd be down here in Arizona working my butt off if I didn't really want to play? I want to play this game badly, and that's the sad thing about it."

McGwire's comments were surprising because he rarely had been so outspoken, and what upset La Russa was that he thought McGwire should have excluded A's owner Walter Haas from his attacks on owners, considering that Haas had paid him well for most of two years in which he couldn't play because of injuries.

"Mark embarrassed himself," La Russa said. "He made this blanket statement and the least he should have done is to qualify it. For two years he hasn't been productive and I don't know how many owners would not have taken a little shot somewhere. They've never said the first word."

McGwire responded that he did have a tremendous respect for the Haas family and appreciated everything they had done for him. He said his comments were general in nature, not specific.

"I never pointed a finger at the Haases. I wasn't speaking for Mark McGwire; I was speaking for the players. I think Tony and Sandy [Alderson] took it personally, thinking I was ripping the Haases. But it was nothing personal. I've had nothing but great experiences playing for the Haases."

McGwire said Haas was the only person from the A's organization who called him after his second foot operation to see how he was doing and that meant a great deal to him.

"Tony has an opinion on the baseball strike," McGwire said. "He's on management's side. I have an opinion. I'm on the players' side. When I made my statement, I was speaking as a players' union member. This is my ninth year in the big leagues. I think I know what I'm talking about."

When the strike lingered and it appeared quite possible that the regular season would begin with replacement players, McGwire left Arizona and returned home to Southern California and predicted it might be the first summer he had spent on the beach since he was 12 years old.

Luckily, it didn't reach that point, as the owners and players reached a labor settlement. McGwire, however, knew that the two sides still were not completely in agreement and the fans were caught in the middle.

"I know some people will be unhappy about what's gone on," McGwire said. "We're all unhappy with what's gone on here. Nobody's won here. But I don't think I can change people's opinions. If they aren't going to come to the games, we're not going to be able to change their minds. If they're not coming back, there's nothing we can do about it.

"I'll do everything I can to make this game exciting again to get people back. We all have to spend a little more time signing autographs and interacting with the fans. There wasn't a day during the strike when people weren't coming up to me and asking questions and giving their opinions, and I understand all that."

McGwire said he was going to try, however, to prove to fans they should forget about the strike.

"I think people might come around again, but we all need to work at it," he said. "We need a long contract for one. It's got to be six years. Got to be. People can't go through this again. The players can't, the owners can't, and the fans can't."

The strike was good for McGwire in one sense—it meant he didn't have to come to the park and watch when he wasn't able to play. Convinced that his foot was fine after playing soccer with kids in his neighborhood, McGwire was ready to get back on the field.

"I love to compete," he said. "I love to be in pressure situations. When you have to sit there and watch, it's a difficult task to deal with."

The comeback wasn't easy. McGwire changed his diet, eliminating pizza and other fatty foods and concentrating on chicken and fish. He took up a running and conditioning program. Once he starting playing again, he had to overcome tendinitis in his left wrist that made it painful to swing a bat.

"Nothing guarantees it's going to come back quickly," McGwire said. "The thing I have to realize is I have not played a lot of games in the last two years. I have played baseball my whole life, and I have come a long way mentally in this game. So I have some added pluses. You can do all the physical stuff you want in the off-season, but to play the game is a different thing."

McGwire had to deal with more medical problems during the year—he was beaned by a pitch from David Cone that forced him to miss the All-Star game, he suffered a deep bruise on his left foot, and his sore lower back acted up again. He missed a total of 40 of the 144 games in the shortened season.

When he played, however, McGwire turned in record-breaking numbers. He hit 39 homers in just 317 at-bats for a ratio of one homer per 8.1 at-bats, which topped Babe Ruth's mark of one homer per 8.5 at-bats set in 1920. McGwire tied his career-best outburst in Cleveland from his rookie season by hitting five homers (in six at-bats) in a two-game span in Boston. The only other player to hit five homers over consecutive games twice in his career was Ralph Kiner.

The performance actually brought McGwire cheers from the Red Sox faithful in Fenway Park, something he only remembered being accorded a visiting player when Nolan Ryan was on the mound.

Even though it didn't land him on the disabled list, the lowest blow of the year, in McGwire's opinion, was when he was beaned by Cone. The pitch hit him in the helmet and literally almost knocked him out.

"I don't think it matters if it was intentional or not," McGwire said. "The fact is he hit me in the head. It's like saying the drunk driver didn't mean to hit those kids crossing the street. The fact is it happened.

"There is no question in my mind if I wasn't almost knocked out, David Cone wouldn't have finished the game. It doesn't matter if it was Cone or anyone else. I've been hit in the head before where I was aware of what was going on. It wasn't until I was walking into the clubhouse I was aware of what was going on. I wish I was aware of it; then I would have taken care of it."

Trainer Barry Weinberg spent the night at McGwire's house, waking him up every two hours to make certain he had not suffered a concussion.

It was the eighth time McGwire had been hit by a pitch in half the season, and he was upset, much as he had been when he thought pitchers were throwing at him to try to intimidate him after his big rookie year.

"I'm a pretty easygoing guy, but I'm fed up," McGwire said. "It's not like I'm a rookie. It's not like I have to earn respect. I won't say publically what I'm going to do if something happens. But I'm just tired of it."

McGwire was forced to miss the All-Star game in Arlington because doctors didn't want to take any chances with him flying on an airplane. McGwire already had talked about perhaps not going to the game if he was selected, but La Russa thought it was a fitting tribute to show how hard he had worked to come back from his injury-plagued seasons.

Despite the year being a personal success for McGwire, the A's struggled to a fourth-place finish. With the Haas family's sale of the team all but completed, McGwire and teammates knew there would be changes.

It didn't come as a shock, but it saddened him when the first major departure was La Russa, the only manager McGwire had played for in the majors, who left to become manager of the St. Louis Cardinals.

Even though the two had a public dispute during the strike, they had a close personal and professional relationship during their years together. McGwire said La Russa was a big supporter when McGwire was going through his personal problems, including the divorce, in 1988.

It also upset McGwire that one of the A's new owners, Steve Schott (no relation to Cincinnati's Marge), made critical comments about several Oakland players before he had ever met them. Schott talked about having to cut back on the team's payroll and said that might mean trading players like McGwire, Steinbach, and Rickey Henderson. Schott said he prefered to have a young, enthusiastic team that would play hard.

"He's not getting off on the right foot with his key players," McGwire said. "I hear I'm not the only one who's upset. I don't know if he realized what he said, but you have got to have a rapport with your players.

"He's got a big wake-up call coming. The thing that blows me away is you should be in baseball a little longer before saying those things."

McGwire stopped short of asking for a trade, but he said his goal was to play on a winning team again.

"I don't want to be on a loser," he said. "I'm tired of losing."

McGwire had played well enough, and avoided serious injuries, to feel confident as he headed into 1996, no matter if he was with the A's or another team. It had been nine years since he gave up his chance to hit a 50th homer so he could be at his son's birth, and maybe this would be the season to do something about it.

12

FIFTY, FINALLY

McGwire knew it was going to take time to adjust to all of the changes the A's had made. Art Howe had replaced La Russa, and the new owners were still to make their presence felt. Some old friends like Todd Stottlemyre and Dennis Eckersley and the coaching staff had joined La Russa in St. Louis. McGwire's name had come up in trade discussions over the winter, and at least a couple of deals, to San Diego and to Cleveland, were a possibility but never materialized.

"It didn't happen, so there isn't anything I can do about it," McGwire said.

Replacing the veterans were younger, unproven players, and McGwire admitted that if he was going to become their leader, the one thing he couldn't do was sit on the bench.

Because of his past history of injuries, Howe's plan was to bring McGwire along slowly to make certain he was ready to go for opening day. Playing in only his seventh game of the spring on March 12, against the Cubs at Mesa, McGwire was trying to score from first on a double by Terry Steinbach in the third inning when he heard a pop in his right heel.

McGwire limped home, but he knew the feeling all too well. Instead of hurting his left foot again, this time he had torn the plantar fascia on his right foot.

"This is just amazing, absolutely amazing," a downtrodden McGwire said.

McGwire had said openly that he didn't think he could endure another lengthy rehabilitation, and the initial projections said this injury could sideline him for three months, maybe until after the All-Star break.

Surrounded by reporters, McGwire said this wasn't the time to talk about retirement, but the subject would be brought up at length in the next few days.

"I'm going to talk to a lot of people, my family and close friends," McGwire said. "I mean, this is just mind-boggling."

The injury stunned McGwire's teammates and his new manager, Howe.

"Everyone is frustrated with it, but the big thing is how he must feel," Steinbach said. "It's one thing if you come in out of shape, but this is a guy who was 100 percent committed to playing and he gets sidelined. I can't begin to fathom how he must feel."

The A's were hoping McGwire had pulled a hamstring muscle, but that wasn't the case.

"I had a sick feeling," Howe said. "I knew he had hurt himself. What are you going to do? You just have to go on."

McGwire said the injury actually would be lessened if he had torn the fascia completely off instead of suffering only a partial tear. He would not have to undergo surgery and would be sidelined for a shorter time.

Still, retirement crossed his mind—until his parents, other relatives, and friends told him that if he retired, he would be making the biggest mistake of his life.

"Everybody was positive," McGwire said. "Everybody left me with the feeling I couldn't walk away from something I had done my whole life if I was going to regret it for the rest of my life."

The thought of retirement had been there before, during his bad season in 1991, during all of the time he spent sidelined in 1993 and 1994, and again when he was hurt in 1995.

"I kept running into a brick wall," McGwire said. "The last brick wall [his latest injury] was huge. I believe I'm just entering my prime. I don't want to waste it. I believe everything happens for a reason. Why this stuff? I'll find out in years to come."

McGwire agreed to undergo the rehab and got

the news he wanted to hear—the fascia was torn completely, meaning there was no need for surgery. The projections for McGwire's return were moved up to May.

While he was recuperating, however, more theories were tossed around about how somebody this dedicated to taking care of his body could keep getting hurt over and over again.

One theory was that he had built himself up too much, adding more bulk and muscles than his arches could support. La Russa seemed to buy into that reasoning.

"Bottom-line, I think he got too strong for his frame," La Russa said. "I want this to come out right, because if he has done anything wrong, he's done it with the best intentions. It's really admirable and not to be criticized, but I think he worked too hard."

McGwire disagreed and said he had consulted with all of the doctors he had seen and none had told him that was the reason.

Dr. Baxter, who had performed both surgeries on McGwire's left foot, said he simply was a victim of bad feet. McGwire said he probably would have suffered the same injury at some point if he were a 185-pound Ping-Pong player and not a 250-pound baseball player.

"It was bad structure given at birth," McGwire said. "It's that simple."

McGwire's dedication to rehabbing the injury got him back on the field in late April, at least a month earlier than expected. He missed only 18 games.

The return was well documented in the Bay Area press, but the fans did not respond for the Tuesday game against Milwaukee. Only 7,026 tickets were sold, and only about 5,000 of those people bothered to come to the game.

"Hey!" Howe couldn't help but yell at McGwire. "I thought you were a big draw here."

McGwire said, "I guess a lot of people got caught in the turnstiles."

The attendance, even if discussed in a joking manner, was a serious situation and one McGwire had addressed when the players' strike finally ended in 1995. Baseball could do all it wanted to try to lure fans back to the park with promotions, special attractions, great games, and even players going for home run records, but the bottom line remained. If the fans didn't want to come, they weren't going to come.

The opposing pitchers had to show up, however, and trying to figure out how to pitch to McGwire, especially when he was in a home run groove, wasn't easy.

"I've sat in on meetings where we had to come up with a game plan for him," said the A's Torey Lovullo, who had also faced McGwire as an opponent. "Then you'd follow your game plan to perfection, and he'd still beat you."

Added teammate Scott Brosius, "He changes the way pitchers throw to the whole lineup. They're not going to want to pitch to him, which will give other guys a chance to drive in some runs."

Baltimore ace Mike Mussina was once asked his

opinion of the best way to pitch to McGwire, and he said, "Low and behind him."

The homers started coming again. McGwire had 11 by the end of May, a warm-up for the 14 he hit in June. Among the June homers were some memorable blasts, and historic ones as well.

At Tiger Stadium, the site of his first career homer a decade earlier, McGwire launched a 462-foot homer that hit the roof in left field. It would have left the park had it not hit a light stand and rolled back. Only three players have ever cleared the roof there—Harmon Killebrew, Frank Howard, and Cecil Fielder.

Howe was asked after the game if he thought the ball was going out. "Out of where?" Howe asked. "Yellowstone?"

At home against Detroit on June 25, McGwire hit two homers—the 300th and 301st of his career. He became the 73rd player in history to reach that milestone.

McGwire's 303rd homer, a week later, July 2, in Seattle, broke the A's all-time homer record dating back to when the franchise began in Philadelphia, a mark that had been set by Jimmie Foxx.

"Most numbers I don't pay attention to," McGwire said. "But these are different. These are good numbers. It says a lot about production and consistency. And it says something about playing in one place for a long time."

One of the other premier home run hitters in the game, Fielder, predicted McGwire was going to hit a lot more before his career finally came to an end.

"Mac's in the best hitting shape of his career," Fielder said. "You haven't seen it all yet. He's got a long way to go. Five hundred homers, maybe more, as long as he stays healthy. For all of us, it all comes down to that."

Lovullo, who had played with Fielder in Detroit before joining the A's, saw a lot of similarities in Fielder's and McGwire's approach to hitting, especially from 1990, the year Fielder hit 51 homers for the Tigers.

"Pitchers work them the same way, trying to bust them inside," Lovullo said. "The problem with that is if you miss by half an inch, they'll kill the pitch. I've watched McGwire all year, and only once have I seen him miss the pitch he's looking for. He missed his pitch and flew out to the warning track. But every other time, it's been a home run. He just doesn't miss."

The home runs had allowed McGwire to forget about his foot and relax. He was enjoying his relationships on the team and had found a new soul mate in 25-year-old Jason Giambi. Reporters even hung the nickname Mac Jr. on Giambi, and that was fine with him.

"He's taught me more than he thinks he has," Giambi said of McGwire. "He's taught me more about the game mentally than physically. He's been one of my biggest fans, saying, 'Hey, kid, it's all right.' He takes care of me, making sure I get to the weight room and making sure I get dinner, things like that."

McGwire said he wasn't doing anything that veteran players hadn't done for him when he was in Giambi's shoes.

"You don't need to influence him at all," McGwire said. "He knows how to play the game. There are guys who are born with the knack and you don't have to say anything to them. He's never intimidated.

"I see a lot of myself in him. He's a great, young, raw talent, but he's yet to adapt to the mental part of the game. I've tried to talk to him about using his mind and pacing himself. Hopefully he won't have to go through the failures that I went through."

McGwire was named the AL Player of the Month for June, recognized for his .329 average, 14 homers, and 25 RBIs. It was the first time in his career he had won the award.

Going to the All-Star game was nothing new for McGwire, and he was named to the team for the 11th time. That also meant another trip to the home run hitting contest, which he had won in San Diego in 1992. McGwire said hitting those eight consecutive homers that day was the first time he ever enjoyed hitting homers in batting practice.

Barry Bonds won the derby at this year's game, in Philadelphia, but the talk among the game's top sluggers wasn't on the contest or the All-Star game; it was about the record and the chase.

All of the names of the leading hitters in the game were mentioned—Ken Griffey Jr., Albert Belle, Frank Thomas, Matt Williams, and others—but the consensus was that if the record was going to fall, McGwire was the favorite to break it.

Nobody said it was going to be easy.

"You don't get the pitches to hit," Thomas said. "I know how it is with me. I get maybe one or two pitches to hit during an at-bat. And if somebody gets that hot and is in a position to challenge it, watch how everybody will pitch around them."

Said Griffey, "It would be hard for a guy to stay locked in for a whole season. You have stretches where you get hot, when you're in a zone, but to do it for that long is tough. And that's saying you're going to stay healthy. Look at me."

Because of his late start to the season, McGwire didn't think this was going to be the year he would challenge the 60-homer barrier. He wanted to know why reporters never discussed how hard it was to get 50 homers.

"People talk about 60 as if 50 doesn't exist," McGwire said. "In all of the years, how many times has it been done? I mean, it's a tremendous feat in itself."

The answer to McGwire's question, through the 1995 season, was 19 times, by 12 different players. Eight of the 12 are in the Hall of Fame; two aren't eligible because they are still playing, Cecil Fielder and Albert Belle. The other two are Maris and George Foster.

Those players might have hit more homers than McGwire, but it's doubtful they hit more long homers.

McGwire closed out July by hitting a bomb into the fifth deck at Toronto's Skydome, which was measured at 488 feet, a distance most observers felt short-changed McGwire.

FIFTY, FINALLY

The blast came off rookie Huck Flener, who said, "You have to take pride in it. I challenge anyone on this team [Toronto] to beat it."

Said Oakland batting coach Denny Walling, "If that isn't 500 feet no ball ever will be."

McGwire's teammate Scott Brosius had the bad timing to miss the blast, having chosen that moment to leave the dugout in pursuit of a soda from the clubhouse. He called it his biggest mistake of the season.

"It's a mistake to ever miss one of his at-bats," Brosius said. "Players usually aren't big fans, but he's a guy you can't help but be in awe of. This guy is the best home run hitter of them all. He's unbelievable."

To check out what he missed, Brosius went up and found the seat that McGwire's ball hit, seven rows into the upper deck, about 150 feet above the playing field.

"You get dizzy just looking down," Brosius said. "The last thing that fan is thinking of is getting a home run ball."

Howe said, "The strength is unbelievable. He's hit balls where other guys need to take cabs to get to. The whole team comes off the bench in amazement when he connects, and they can feel everyone in the park is in amazement. Every town we go into it seems he hits the longest ball hit in that ballpark."

It wasn't just baseballs that McGwire could drive a long way. Former teammate Rick Honeycutt recalled the time he, McGwire, and other teammates played at a golf course near Toronto and McGwire was crushing ball after ball.

"McGwire's buddy Billy Andrade, the golfer, tells a story about one time when they were at the driving range at Pebble Beach," Honeycutt said. "They have a row of pine trees about 275 yards away, and when the pros come into town they routinely hit drives into those trees. Andrade said Mark was hitting there one day and the whole range just stopped to watch. He was hitting balls that were going 50 to 60 feet over the trees. Finally there was a little squeaky voice from behind where everybody was watching and this guy said, 'Pretty good little swing you've got there.' Andrade and McGwire turned around and saw the guy was Jack Nicklaus."

The talk about all of the long homers, like the Maris record chase, bothered McGwire.

"When I broke in they didn't keep track of things the way they do now," he said. "These days they have a stat for how many times a guy goes for a cup of coffee."

McGwire finished July with 38 homers, and his eight in August left him at 46 entering September. His homer on August 13 marked the end of a 162-game stretch, dating back to the previous June, during which he hit 70 homers.

He hit numbers 47 and 48 in back-to-back games against Kansas City and went into a doubleheader at Cleveland on September 14 needing one to tie his personal best and two to reach the coveted 50-homer plateau.

The first mark fell in the first inning of the first game, and he didn't have to wait long to get the next.

It came in the first inning of the second game off Chad Ogea, landing in the third row of the left field bleachers.

"This was one of the most special moments of my career," McGwire said. "I wasn't supposed to play until the All-Star break, and now I have 50 home runs."

Said Howe, "You could see it in his eyes. He's not a guy who shows any emotion, so when he does, you know how special it was and how important it was to him."

Running around the bases, McGwire knew the next thing he had to do—he went in the clubhouse and called his son, Matthew, in California.

"He wasn't home," McGwire said. "He was on the golf course. I talked to his mom [Kathy, his ex-wife]. She was excited, and I know Matthew will be, too."

The home run ball was caught by 11-year-old Adam Ulm of North Canton, Ohio, who exchanged it for a team ball autographed by the A's and another autographed just by McGwire. The special ball was hand-delivered to Matthew two days later.

McGwire has never been a collector of memorabilia, his or anyone's. His home in Southern California is filled with pictures, mostly of Matthew, but there is very little evidence that a professional baseball player lives there.

McGwire hit two more homers before the year ended, both in the same inning at the Kingdome in Seattle, finishing the year with 52 homers. He also finished the year with a .312 batting average, 23 points better than the .289 he hit as a rookie.

Especially considering how his year had begun, he didn't see how it could be any better. If anyone was disappointed that he had not broken Maris's record, it certainly wasn't McGwire.

"Someday somebody is going to break the home run record, and it will be an unbelievable feat," McGwire said. "I don't sit here thinking about it because I realize how difficult it is.

"I mean, hitting a home run is probably the most difficult thing in sports, and doing it consistently in the second half of a season when teams aren't pitching to you is mind-boggling."

Steinbach knew how much pitchers were working around McGwire, and he said he could only imagine what it would be like if the record was closer to falling.

"The one thing I can relate it to is pitchers who pitched to Cal [Ripken] last year [during his streak to beat Lou Gehrig's record]," Steinbach said. "No one in his right mind wanted to hit him or knock him out of the game. Flip-flop it. Who wants to be known for giving that up to Mac? He gets pitched around a lot now. Imagine if he gets to 55 or 57."

Perhaps because of his injured start, there wasn't as much talk about McGwire going after Maris's record this year, except in the New York media, and that contributed to what McGwire said was one of the best years he had enjoyed in his career.

He was able to stay positive, he was able to stay focused, and he was able to laugh and smile. Those feelings sometimes don't come as easily for a lot of major leaguers as you might think, McGwire said.

"There are pro ballplayers who are not happy inside," McGwire said. "There are a lot of people in general who can't look themselves in the mirror and say, 'I like myself.'"

McGwire admits he would not have been able to say that years earlier or without the help of his counseling sessions.

"I'm not the only athlete to see a therapist," he said. "Others treat it like it makes them less of a person and hide it. There's absolutely nothing weak about it. It should be viewed as a strength, because you're willing to deal with real-life problems.

"Without my counseling sessions, I would never have made it to where I am this day. I'm so much stronger mentally than what people see physically."

McGwire's mental strength had been challenged before, but a new, harder test was coming.

13

THE END OF AN ERA

Thinking here were more trade rumors over the winter. McGwire, going into the final year of his contract, knew the A's were in a quandary about what to do with him. As much as Sandy Alderson and the rest of the team hierarchy admired McGwire and what he had accomplished in his career, did it really make sense to re-sign him to a huge contract when the rest of the team figured to be young and inexperienced, meaning there was little chance of winning the pennant?

If the A's had already decided that McGwire was not going to be re-signed, did it make sense to trade him before the year began? The only catch in that scenario was that McGwire, as a player with 10 years in the majors and more than five with the same club, had to approve any deal.

Would McGwire accept less than market value to stay in Oakland? That was another possibility.

"I've given them no guarantees, but I'll be more than happy to listen," McGwire said.

The one absolute rule laid down by McGwire and his agent over the winter was that they would not negotiate during the season. If no agreement or trade was reached before the regular season began, McGwire would play out his contract and become a free agent at the end of the year.

McGwire watched more good players and friends leave as Steinbach signed with the Twins and shortstop Mike Bordick went to Baltimore. As much as McGwire said he would like to stay in Oakland, losing players like that made him question management's commitment to winning. Playing on a team in pursuit of a pennant was going to be McGwire's biggest consideration when it came to deciding his future.

"We have great young talent; there's no doubt about that," McGwire said. "But you must have certain [veteran] players so the young talent can blend in. I hope to God we get some people or it's going to be another learning year. Last year was a nice learning year, but you're not supposed to go backward. You've got to concentrate on going forward. At this point we've taken a step backward."

The A's did add a player McGwire was familiar

with before spring training, trading pitcher John Wasdin to the Red Sox to reacquire Jose Canseco.

As much as McGwire had enjoyed their earlier relationship and the success he and Canseco both had achieved together, McGwire's biggest concern was that Canseco didn't play shortstop, catch, or pitch, the three areas he thought were in the biggest need of improvement.

Before reporting to Arizona, McGwire, Bordick, and Steinbach, all of whom had played in Modesto in their minor-league careers, helped start a fund-raising campaign to help victims of a massive flood in that city. The three contributed $20,000, and other collection efforts led to the A's presenting a check to Modesto officials for $120,000.

Mayor Dick Lang said the money would be used for temporary housing, transportation, and counseling for flood victims.

As McGwire drove across the desert to spring training, he had some time to consider his future. Knowing more teams trained in Florida, he wondered if this would be the last time he would make this trip. Where would he be playing at this time next year? It was going to be entirely his call, which put him in a nice position, but he also didn't like the uncertainty his contract status created.

Awaiting him in Arizona was a media frenzy about the reunion of the Bash Brothers, McGwire and Canseco. The media had never understood how totally different the two of them were, connected only by the fact they both had been young, quality hitters playing on the same team.

THE END OF AN ERA

The A's had even tried to re-create the Bash Brothers theme in their advertising campaign for the 1997 season, but McGwire would have no part of that.

"Mark had them change it," said Ted Polakowski, who was there when the commericals were being shot. "He said he didn't want anything about the Bash Brothers. He said they were not the same two people they were back then."

Canseco had moved on from Texas to Boston and had enjoyed some quality seasons but hadn't come close to matching his performance in Oakland when most scouts predicted that he, not McGwire, was going to develop into the team's franchise player and resident superstar.

"We really didn't know each other personally, and we never hung out," McGwire said. "People just associate us because of all the Bash Brothers stuff. That was a big thing for the A's at a time when the team was winning.

"Things have changed. We're older; we're wiser; we're the veterans—that's really the big difference. We've come a long way. To think we'd ever play to-gether again, well, it's surprising."

McGwire said he could tell early in their reunion that Canseco had toned down his lifestyle and was not the same flamboyant, shoot-from-the-hip and damn-the-consequences kind of guy that he had been a decade earlier.

"Nobody really knew Jose before," McGwire said. "He was always in his own world. He didn't let

191

anybody know him. That was his personality, but I can see in the way he relates to people now that he's changed, grown, matured. I think it's going to be fun having him back."

For his part, Canseco said he was glad to be back and reunited with McGwire. Canseco was victimized by injuries, like McGwire, during his stints in Texas and Boston, and he said the key to each of their performances, and that of the club, would be determined by health.

"To me, Mark is the best power hitter in baseball," Canseco said. "He's going to break the record [61 homers]. To hit 52 while missing a month is amazing, but he's developed to a point where he can do it every year. He's so strong, so consistent, and knows the game so well.

"If we both get 500 to 600 at-bats, it will be something to watch. The question with us is health. You can't put up numbers from the disabled list."

Seeing both McGwire and Canseco together in the same clubhouse reminded Polakowski that he had some old jerseys he wanted to get signed. When the Huntsville minor-league team had changed jerseys a few years earlier, he had asked Alderson what he wanted him to do with the old ones. They decided to save a few, like the ones worn by McGwire, Canseco, and a few other players, and get rid of the rest.

Polakowski had stored them away but got them out for McGwire and Canseco to autograph. McGwire had worn number 33 when he played in

Huntsville in 1986, while Canseco had worn number 44 a year earlier.

"I got the jersey out for Mark, and he looked all surprised. 'You've got it,' he said. When I asked him why he was so surprised, he said, 'Some guy in Kansas City keeps bringing me a Huntsville jersey with number 25 on it and I won't sign it because I didn't wear number 25 there. I kept telling him it wasn't my jersey. You had it the whole time.'"

McGwire did sign this jersey, as did Canseco, and they now are framed and hanging on the wall of the A's Arizona complex.

Polakowski said it was a good thing McGwire didn't try to slip the jersey on for old times' sake—it was a size 44, and he now wears a size 52, one indication of how much muscle he has added over the years.

Nothing happened on McGwire's contract front before spring training ended, and he began the year trying to stay focused on just playing as well as he could.

It helped that he got off to a blazing start, hitting 11 homers in April, including another shot at Detroit that this time did clear the roof in left field. The homer was measured at 514 feet.

In Cleveland, McGwire closed out the month by hitting the longest homer ever at Jacobs Field, a 488-foot bolt off the scoreboard in left center that put a dent in between the "e" and the "i" in the Budweiser sign.

As McGwire crossed home plate catcher Sandy

Alomar asked him if he wanted the ball, but he said no. McGwire said he lost track of it off his bat and didn't see where it hit.

As he had told Reggie Jackson after that long homer at Fenway Park in Boston during the tour of the U.S. Olympic team, McGwire doesn't stand and watch his homers. McGwire considers that an act of trying to show up the pitcher.

"I never have and I never will," he said. "When I was a youngster I was taught not to be in awe of anything, but to respect people. I have a lot of respect for the pitcher I am facing. He is doing his best to get me out, and I am doing all I can to get a hit off him.

"Hitting a home run and standing there is showing a lack of respect. When I was growing up and playing baseball, no one ever did that. Now, young kids see players showing pitchers up and think it's the thing to do.

"To me, it's upsetting to see what some of these kids in high school and college do. All we're talking about here is one at-bat."

After hitting his blast in Cleveland, the first to reach the scoreboard there, McGwire lifted weights for 30 minutes and then returned to his locker, surprised to see 25 reporters still standing there waiting for him.

"It is embarrassing," McGwire said. "There are so many players in the game who do the same thing I do."

Most people would dispute McGwire on that statement, including his manager.

"He comes to play every day," Howe said. "He loves to play. He is just a quality human being, someone who does a lot of things off the field with kids. After every game, he is always throwing batting gloves to kids. A lot of the things he does go unnoticed.

"He downplays everything. I know when it is all said and done, though, he is going to be able to say he's accomplished some nice things."

After the game, McGwire found a 12-pack of Budweiser at his locker, autographed by the Indians' Jim Thome. "Mac, this Bud's for you," the note said. McGwire took the memento home and has never opened it.

"When Mac hit that ball, it got us all excited," Canseco said. "I think everyone would like to hit a ball that far, just to see what it would be like. But Mac's the only one capable of doing that. It's hard enough in batting practice, but to actually do it in game situations is extremely difficult."

A longer homer was coming. On June 24, in a game against the Mariners in the Kingdome, McGwire redirected a 97-mph fastball from former USC teammate Randy Johnson and sent a rocket 538 feet into the upper deck. It landed just six rows away from the back of the seating area. That was the longest home run ever recorded since the measurement of homers was established as a formal major-league program in 1992.

"I didn't know if I should meet him at home plate," Johnson said. "It probably should have counted for two runs."

What was more incredible about the homer was that it came on a night when Johnson was striking out 19 batters, just one off the major-league record.

That blast was McGwire's 27th of the season. He reached the All-Star break with 31 homers—halfway to the record—and was selected to the AL squad for the ninth time. He went 0-for-2 in the game, increasing his career All-Star total to 16 at-bats without a homer.

There was more for reporters to talk and write about as the second half of the season began than McGwire's record chase. Was he going to have a shot at the record in Oakland, or was he going to be playing somewhere else?

The deadline for trading a player without having to first obtain waivers was July 31, so McGwire knew that was the time frame the A's were working against. If he wasn't dealt by then, he knew he would finish the season in Oakland and then become a free agent.

There were days when McGwire thought he was going to be traded, followed by days when he thought he would be staying. The confusion and the uneasiness of the situation began to play games in his head and started to affect his performance on the field.

A month before the deadline, the only teams that had called Oakland about McGwire were Toronto and St. Louis. If McGwire was going to pick his new team, he wanted to go where he could be closer to his son, Matthew, during the summer as well as the winter.

"I want to be around him more than I am," Mc-Gwire said. "We've always been close, but we've been even closer since he's become more self-sufficient. We play golf together; we go to the movies together; we do everything together.

"It's the greatest joy in my life, spending time with him, hands down. We're so much alike. I look at him and it's like I'm looking in a mirror. He knows that I want to be close to him. He knows I want to be near him every day."

Two teams would have fit McGwire's desire to be in the Los Angeles area, the Angels and the Dodgers, but neither seemed interested in McGwire. As the deadline inched closer, maybe that would change.

McGwire still wasn't convinced he was going anywhere, anyway.

"If Sandy Alderson comes to me and says there's a possibility of a trade, then I'd listen to that. I never said I would OK a trade. It would all depend," McGwire said.

Alderson, while facing the question of 1998 and beyond, also had to worry about the fan reaction in 1997 if he traded McGwire. He well could spend August and September marching toward 60 homers, and how many people would that put in the Oakland Coliseum? Without McGwire, and without a home run record chase, and without any realistic hope of being in a pennant race, Alderson knew attendance would be very sparse.

"It's another consideration," Alderson admitted.

"We sold a lot of tickets based on Mark McGwire being part of the team. If he's on pace to hit 60 home runs in July, is it fair to trade him? The caveat is: He was on pace to hit 60 last year and no one came out to see him. And the same people who bought those tickets to see him want the club to get better."

Watching the situation developing from St. Louis was La Russa, who wanted nothing better than to be able to write McGwire's name onto his lineup card again.

"I don't see how we've got a shot," La Russa said in mid-July, two weeks before the deadline. "If you trade them something not knowing you're going to keep him . . . hopefully we've got better sense than that."

That, of course, was the other factor in any potential trade discussion. As a pending free agent, McGwire would be free to leave his new team and move on again over the winter, leaving the club that had traded him with only an amateur draft pick in return. No club would trade a group of good prospects, which was what the A's were looking for, without some kind of commitment from McGwire that he would re-sign with them.

After coming so close to free agency, and knowing in his heart that he would like to play in Southern California, McGwire was not willing to make that commitment.

The deadline was approaching. The talks between the A's and the Cardinals grew serious when it appeared no other teams were going to make an offer. Oakland asked about some of the Cardinals' young players, like minor-league pitcher Braden Looper, catcher Eli Marrero, and shortstop Brent Butler. Names like those of young pitchers Matt Morris and Alan Benes were thrown around, but Alderson knew that Cardinals GM Walt Jocketty would not let one of those two loose.

McGwire heard the rumors and knew the discussions were going on. As much as he tried to block it out of his mind, it stayed there, 24 hours a day, when he was playing the game and when he was at home. He hit two homers on July 16 against Kansas City, his 33rd and 34th of the season. But he didn't homer again the rest of the month.

Even if the A's and Cardinals agreed on the players to be involved in the deal, what would McGwire say? He was leery of going to the National League, especially in the middle of the season, when he still had a mathematical shot at Maris's record.

As he thought more and more about it, however, McGwire began to look at the possibility of going to the National League as a challenge.

By July 30, the day before the deadline, the two sides still were far apart. McGwire finished a series with the A's in New York and took a cross-country flight back to Oakland. The Cardinals completed a series in Houston and moved on to Philadelphia, trailing the first-place Astros by seven games in the NL Central.

"He's stubborn," La Russa said of Alderson, his former boss. "He's an ex-marine. He's got a lot of principle, and I admire him."

McGwire had made up his mind a few days earlier that if the A's and Cardinals could reach an agreement on the players involved, he would OK the deal. He wasn't really risking much, he finally decided, since it was only for two months and he would still be free to sign with whatever team he wanted over the winter.

Maybe his presence would help the Cardinals get back into the pennant race, and that prospect certainly wasn't going to happen this year in Oakland.

Jocketty and Alderson burned up the telephone lines before finally the deal was done, just a few hours before the midnight deadline. McGwire was traded to the Cardinals for pitchers T. J. Mathews, Eric Ludwick, and Blake Stein.

McGwire got the news in a telephone call from his agent as he was driving across the Bay Bridge from his home in San Francisco to Oakland for the A's game that night.

He got a little emotional during a news conference in Oakland, but after he cleaned out his locker and left the stadium for the final time he knew he had made the right decision. As had always been his custom in baseball and life, he was looking ahead, not backward.

"These were 11 years of a lot of great times," McGwire said. "I had some down times personally, but like Sandy said, I grew up in this organization. This was not an easy decision, but sometimes you come to a crossroads in your life, when change might be good for you. I came to that crossroads.

"It's going to be a challenge, and to tell you the truth, I think that's what I need. That's why I decided to do this, the challenge and for a change. I've always had a great work ethic, and I'll just keep doing the things I've always done and try to put some numbers up for the Cardinals."

Even though the deal had been weeks in the making, the fact that it actually happened came as something of a surprise.

"I'll admit that, right now, it's probably the saddest day of my career," Giambi said. "You don't replace a guy like that. He took me under his wing and taught me how to play the game.

"I'm happy for him. He gets a chance to go play for a winner. It was killing him inside to come to the park and try to find new [goals] to play for. It's tough when you're a guy who's gone through all those winning years."

Said Alderson, "You never feel as if you get enough in any trade. We're happy with the three players we obtained. We got a major-league pitcher, and the two prospects are power arms. Certainly what we obtained for Mark was more than we could have gotten had he become a free agent at the end of the season."

McGwire left Oakland as the A's franchise leader in homers, with 363, RBIs, extra-base hits, and slugging percentage. The city and the organization had been good to him, and he had returned the favor.

McGwire was looking ahead again, not behind, as he left Oakland. He returned to his home in San Francisco, packed some more of his belongings, tried to sleep for a few hours, and then left for the airport to catch an 8:00 A.M. flight to join the Cardinals in Philadelphia.

14

A CONTENTED CARDINAL

The Cardinals were a little surprised when the deal was actually completed. At about 6:30 P.M. on July 31, five and a half hours before the trading deadline, Jocketty didn't think the A's were going to go along with his idea of substituting Ludwick for Manny Aybar in the trade.

"We were looking at a number of other hitters," Jocketty said, well aware that the Cardinals had been limited to two runs or less 41 times already in the season. "We were determined to get a quality bat in the middle of our lineup, and I think we got the best hitter we could."

Alderson finally got back to Jocketty and said OK—if the Cardinals put Ludwick in the package with T. J. Mathews and Blake Stein, they had a deal.

Jocketty knew he was taking a gamble that could backfire two months later. McGwire could decide he wanted to play in Southern California and depart as a free agent, leaving the Cardinals with nothing more than an extra pick in the amateur draft.

Jocketty was hedging his bet, however, that the only realistic chance the Cardinals had of signing Mc-Gwire as a free agent was to get him in St. Louis, playing for two months, to sample what the team and the city were like. He had never played there and thus only knew what he saw on television, read in the media, and heard from other players.

"When he sees what a quality baseball environment it is—with the organization, with the stadium we have and most of all the fans—I think when he gets there, he's going to be surprised how great it really is," Jocketty said.

The trade, surprisingly, was not met with unanimous approval in St. Louis. Writing in the *St. Louis Post-Dispatch* the next morning, columnist Bernie Miklasz quoted Jocketty as saying, "Mark McGwire will make a huge difference in the middle of our lineup." Miklasz then wrote: "Wrong. McGwire will be huge, yes. A huge difference, no. Jocketty should have thought of the long-range future instead of taking a short-term risk. And if he wanted to think big, he should have pursued Seattle's baby bull, Jose Cruz, Jr."

Miklasz tried to make a comparison between the Cardinals getting McGwire and the NHL St. Louis Blues making a deal a year earlier for Wayne Gretzky, who was in a similar position of pending free agency. Gretzky did well in St. Louis but got into a feud with coach-GM Mike Keenan and left for the New York Rangers.

Miklasz predicted the same thing, although not the feud, would happen with McGwire.

"We'll all wonder why the Cardinals, like the Blues, sacrificed a promising piece of tomorrow for instant—but ultimately unsatisfying—gratification," Miklasz wrote. "The Cardinals, like the Blues with Wayne Gretzky, will provide temporary shelter for a free-agent celebrity.

"McGwire will pad his resume with a few homers, then strut away to collect a ransom of free-agent millions this offseason. Unless the Cardinals want to flirt with financial calamity by offering McGwire the largest contract in baseball history, he will bolt."

That kind of column illustrates what McGwire and other players say is a problem of the media. If Miklasz had ever met McGwire or done an interview with him, it was in a packed-room setting at the World Series or the All-Star game. Miklasz didn't know McGwire personally, didn't know what made McGwire different from other players, and didn't know how wrong he would turn out to be.

The feeling in the Cardinals' locker room, especially from McGwire's former teammates in Oakland and ex–American Leaguers who had played against him, was entirely different.

"He's probably the greatest power hitter of all time," said pitcher Todd Stottlemyre. "And, besides, that, he's a great person.

"If you're a Cardinal fan and you don't know what to think about him, by the time you see him launch balls out of the ballpark you'll get pretty excited about it. I'm sure there's 27 other teams that could find room for him. He could fit in on any ball club."

Said La Russa, "The one thing he does that's the most impressive thing he does is talk to the other guys about the right way to be a professional winning player. He'll go to them and talk to them about things like taking a pitch when the team is behind, playing through minor injuries, hitting to the opposite field. And he likes to talk to, teach, and really get involved with the young players."

After his second cross-country flight in three days, McGwire arrived in Philadelphia about 90 minutes before game time. Batting coach George Hendrick, who had worn number 25 since he played for the Cardinals in 1980 and later as an instructor, agreed to switch to number 21 so McGwire could keep his familar number.

McGwire's debut lacked any heroics—he went 0-for-3 with a walk—as the Cardinals lost their fourth straight, 4–1.

McGwire said the strangest part of his NL debut was putting on the Cardinals' red shoes. He had been wearing white since 1984.

After splitting two more games in Philadelphia, the Cardinals played two games in New York and two in Atlanta, all losses, before returning home for McGwire to make his St. Louis debut on August 8.

Perhaps because he was still adjusting to all the changes, the road trip had not gotten him off to a great start. He failed to hit a homer, extending his streak of at-bats without a homer, dating back to his last two weeks in Oakland, to 71—the second longest drought of his career—including his first 27 as a Cardinal.

That all changed in the third inning of his first game in St. Louis when, pumped up by the cheers of an extra 7,100 people who bought tickets to see his first game at Busch Stadium, McGwire pulled a pitch from Philadelphia's Mark Leiter down the left field line, where it hit the foul pole about at the height of the Stadium Club. The shot was estimated at 441 feet.

During his first batting practice session in St. Louis, McGwire had been surprised so many fans came out early to watch him hit. He didn't disappoint the faithful either, as he hit 11 homers out of the 26 pitches that he saw.

McGwire had been in St. Louis only once before, as part of the U.S. team's tour in 1983. He hit a homer in one of the two games the team played against Korea, but that homer, a three-run shot in the ninth that gave the U.S. a 6–4 win, came at ABC Park in north St. Louis County.

"This is all a learning process," McGwire said. "It might be easier for a pitcher to switch leagues than for a hitter. I'm big into visualization before every at-bat. To do that for the first time you face a pitcher, that's hard. It has not been an easy adjustment."

McGwire said one of the hardest adjustments

came in the different batter's boxes, as he tried to feel comfortable at the plate. For McGwire, a big part of his success comes when he feels comfortable and relaxed, being able to visualize the pitches and paint a picture with his mind about what he is trying to do in that at-bat.

The reaction from the St. Louis fans—cheering when he stepped on the field, cheering when he hit a batting practice homer into the upper deck, cheering even when he struck out during the game—was something McGwire had never experienced before. In some ways, it could have made him even more nervous than he was, trying too hard to please all of those fans.

For McGwire, though, it worked in the other direction. He felt accepted and wanted, and in such a short period of time he had a hard time coming to grips with it all. This was not what he had expected to happen. He had fully intended to play out the two months, get a feel for the National League, and then decide what he wanted to do with his future.

The more he thought about it, and as more homers began to come again in August and early September, the more he began to visualize himself staying in St. Louis. Matthew came to visit for a week, and he also felt at ease in the city, which would be a big part of McGwire's decision.

Even as he went around the National League, he was beginning to feel more and more comfortable— except with the media and fans' sudden interest in how many homers he hit in batting practice and how far they went.

In Colorado, he hit one during BP that landed in the players' parking lot and was estimated at 568 feet.

"I wish people would stop writing about that," McGwire said. "I don't know why the fascination with batting practice has become a big deal. What it does is draw attention, which is something I don't really want. I'm the type of person where what people don't know goes on won't hurt them. This is drawing attention to the pitchers that I'm facing, and I don't like that.

"They don't need to know that I've hit 'x' amount of home runs in batting practice. Batting practice is meaningless. It doesn't mean that I'm going to get a hit in the game."

Even some of his teammates and opponents, however, didn't view McGwire's prodigious pokes in batting practice as meaningless. Catcher Tom Pagnozzi even asked pitching coach Dave Duncan to reschedule the nightly pitchers' meeting, which had been during McGwire's batting practice time, so they could watch him hit.

"It's really fun to watch," said third baseman Gary Gaetti, "the anticipation of 'how far is this one going?' I think it would be better to get him an aluminum bat and see how far he could hit it. But you'd have to clear everyone off the field. And you'd have to warn the fans, 'He's using an aluminum bat. We're not responsible for his actions.'"

McGwire hit nine homers in August, raising his season total to 43. Eighteen behind Maris with 26 games to play meant long odds, and that might have helped McGwire relax a little more. His real goal was to get to 50, becoming the only hitter other than Ruth to hit 50 or more homers in consecutive seasons. Ruth did it twice, following up his 60-homer season in 1927 with 54 in 1928. He also had done it earlier, hitting 54 in 1920 and 59 the following year.

A four-homer outburst in three games at Colorado increased McGwire's total to 48 as the Cardinals headed to San Francisco, across the bay from his former team in Oakland. He hit his 49th homer on September 9 and didn't have to wait long for the magic 50th, connecting the next day.

McGwire said it had special meaning for him to hit the homer in San Francisco, in front of many of the same fans who had been cheering for him for years in Oakland. He received a standing ovation from the crowd after the 446-foot blast into the lower deck in left field.

"I had the confidence that sooner or later it was going to happen," said McGwire, who added that when the ball left his bat he said to himself, "I did it; I did it."

McGwire made a point of retrieving the ball as he had his 50th homer of the previous year. The ball was caught by a man named Scott Ford, who had left his seat to make a trip to the concession stand. McGwire autographed two bats in exchange for the ball and inscribed the one to Ford: "How was your beer?"

McGwire had been in St. Louis only slightly more than a month, but he had reached a decision—he wanted to stay. He called up his agent,

Cohen, and instructed him to see if he could get the deal completed. The stunned Cohen tried to talk Mc-Gwire out of it, saying he should wait until the off-season, just to gauge the interest of other teams. The Angels would surely make an offer, and Cohen said he had reason to believe they would hear from the Braves. Cohen told McGwire to sleep on it, but the next morning McGwire's decision hadn't changed.

On September 16, the negotiations were complete and McGwire signed a three-year contract worth an estimated $28.5 million that also included an option for a fourth year.

If that news wasn't enough to make Cardinals fans giddy, what happened at the press conference to announce the deal put McGwire into their hearts forever.

One provision of the contract was that McGwire agreed to donate $1 million a year to a new charitable foundation for children who had been sexually and physically abused.

When asked a question about the new foundation, McGwire started crying and had to stop talking. He was silent for 33 seconds as he tried to comprehend everything that had happened to him in the previous six weeks.

"I'm definitely overwhelmed with the contract," said McGwire, despite the fact that he might have received more money on the open market. "I don't think it was too hard to fall in love with St. Louis. This is what everybody was talking about when I came over. I'll tell you what—it makes me float every time I come to the ballpark and play in front of these fans. I've never been treated that way as a baseball player. This is just unbelievable."

The fans in Busch Stadium were buzzing about the contract when McGwire came to bat in the first inning of that night's game against the Dodgers. They were on their feet with a resounding standing ovation as McGwire stepped into the batter's box, and they didn't stop cheering through the entire at-bat.

McGwire worked the count against Ramon Martinez to 3–1, then launched a 517-foot rocket off the facade above the scoreboard in left center field, at the time the longest home run in stadium history.

"Look what he just did!" yelled radio broadcaster Jack Buck on the air. "Look what he just did!"

In his column in the *Post-Dispatch* the following morning, Miklasz admitted that McGwire was different from most athletes and Jocketty had, in fact, made a good trade.

"This just isn't supposed to happen in professional sports," Miklasz wrote. "We have come to expect greed, lies, phonies. We are not accustomed to happy endings. Athletes come, athletes go. They chase the buck. They auction themselves to the highest bidder. They break the bank. They break hearts.

"They go. They change uniforms. Before we can consider them part of the family, they are long gone, adopted by a new rich man. You show them the money, and they leave. The dollar sign always wins. The fans lose.

"McGwire was different, refreshingly so. He was a man of honor."

A CONTENTED CARDINAL

The difference was that McGwire put his personal happiness above the power of seeking the most money he could find, regardless of where that turned out to be. He hoped he was sending a message to other athletes.

"I hope more players feel the way I feel," McGwire said. "Granted, there's a lot of money out there, and you've always thought of getting as much as you can because you don't know how long your career is going to last.

"But you know, if you're happy at a place, for you to take less dollars . . . Well, I think the first and foremost thing in the game of baseball is you've got to be happy with yourself. There's a lot of people out there making a lot of money and they're not very happy. I'm the first one to tell you right now that I'm very happy."

Part of his happiness came because he finally felt he was able to make a significant contribution to society through his foundation.

"People have asked me to do things throughout my career and I didn't think I was ready," McGwire said. "I think now I'm in a position where I am. Whatever it takes and however long it takes to get this thing up and running, I will do it."

McGwire said he had no personal experience with physically or sexually abused children when he was growing up but had become aware of how widespread the problem was through some friends he had met in the past few years. Now he can't watch a group of children playing in a school yard or on a Little

League field and fail to wonder how many of them are being abused. The thought sickens him.

"Things happen to children, and they don't know what's going on, and then they grow up into teenagers and young adults, and the way they were raised is the way they raise their children," McGwire said. "There are so many issues to touch on; I want to do what I can to make people aware of what's happening.

"If young people have this happen to them, and we are able to take this to the forefront and give them a place to talk about this, we can improve their lives. Children who are raised with sexual and physical abuse, they wonder why they're not able to do X, Y, and Z when they're grown up. It's because their past history is sunken down in the pit of their stomachs. They can't break out unless they get help. That helps them be a better person, a better adult.

"There's so much awareness about abuse, but it still happens. Will it ever stop? It will probably never stop. Can we make a dent in it, make people more aware? Yes, we can."

The fact that McGwire had signed his new contract and included such a provision didn't surprise those who had known him for a long time, like Stottlemyre, or those who had recently gotten to know him, like shortstop Royce Clayton.

"It says a lot about him and his character that he signed," Stottlemyre said. "He could have waited one more month, and I couldn't imagine a better situation for a player to test the waters. He could have waited a month and who knows what would have happened? Maybe he could have owned the team.

"He's something this organization and this city can be proud of. I'm happy for Mark. As much as the city deserves a player like Mark McGwire, he deserves a city like this, too."

Said Clayton, "All the things you heard about Mark before he came here were true. But the one thing we didn't hear enough about was the type of person and the great individual that he is."

The blast against the Dodgers was McGwire's 52nd homer of the year, tying the career high he had established in 1996. McGwire wasn't ready to stop there.

He went on to hit 15 homers in September, breaking the Cardinals' record for most homers in a month, which had stood since Whitey Kurowski hit 12 in August 1947.

McGwire finished the year with 58 homers, the highest in the majors since Maris's 61. He tied Jimmie Foxx and Hank Greenberg for the most homers by a right-handed batter, and his two-year total of 110 also set a record for a right-handed hitter.

It had been a long year and had turned out far differently than McGwire would have predicted when he drove across the Arizona desert to spring training. He was ready to relax over the winter, then begin to prepare himself for another season.

What, he wondered, would happen in 1998?

15

AN ENCORE PERFORMANCE

For all of the years that McGwire had been playing in the majors, never did he come into a season with as much anticipation as he did in 1998.

In his second year, after a stellar rookie campaign, people were curious about he would do, but most didn't really expect him to hit 49 homers again. After all of his injury-filled seasons, people just wondered when McGwire would break down again, not how many homers he would hit.

When he got healthy again in 1996, people expected a good year the following season, but 1997 had the free-agency cloud hanging over it that people knew might alter McGwire's performance.

He had no such problems entering 1998. McGwire was happy and content with a new contract in a place he quickly had grown to love, playing on a team that he expected to contend for the National League pennant, and all the signs were there for him to have a splendid year.

"It wasn't until I got to St. Louis last year that I really got to know and understand the passion fans have for baseball," McGwire said. "When the baseball season starts in St. Louis, they bleed red. Everybody told me I'd love St. Louis, and no wonder. This franchise is absolutely amazing in all it's accomplished, all the pennants they've won and the Hall of Famers they've turned out."

About the only part of the anticipation that Mc-Gwire didn't like as the Cardinals reported to their new spring training home in Jupiter, Florida, was the personal attention focused on him, not the team.

"I know there's a lot of eyes on me," McGwire said.

Those eyes were watching for one reason, to see if this would be the season he could top the 61-homer barrier. McGwire has never predicted that he would break the record, but he said hitting 58 in 1997 despite the trade and hitting only five homers in July convinced him the record could be broken.

"It's made baseball a little more exciting to think about it and talk about it," McGwire said in the spring. "But if you really look at it, ever since I was a kid, what do you go to the ballpark for? You go to the ballpark to see somebody hit a home run or somebody throw a ball at close to 100 miles an hour. That was the exciting thing when I was a kid, and I think it still is."

McGwire doesn't understand, however, why there is more talk about the record now than there was during all of his years in Oakland. Perhaps it was because before 1998, he never had been at the proper place, at the proper time in his life, to mount the challenge to the record.

McGwire has often said that a home run is a base hit that happens to leave the ballpark. There are very few times, he said, when he goes to the plate actually trying to hit a home run. It is just the mechanics of his swing, combined with his strength and power, that often means the ball is going over the fence if he connects.

"I really believe hitting home runs is a God-given talent," McGwire said. "Every year adults ask me, 'Can you teach my son how to hit home runs?' And I say, 'No, I can't.' I think you're given the talent. If you want to work on it, then you become a successful baseball player. It's just a tough thing."

Several factors were combining in the 1998 season to make most observers believe McGwire, Ken Griffey Jr., Sammy Sosa, or some other hitter would be able to mount a challenge to the record. Another expansion, adding teams in Arizona and Tampa Bay, had further diluted the spotty pitching already in the majors. The lively ball was expected to be just as lively in 1998, and the confidence level of hitters like McGwire and Griffey had never been higher.

"I'm a firm believer that you have to be happy with yourself and happy with what you're doing; then you can appreciate things," McGwire said. "I can't stand being around people who are negative."

McGwire didn't waste any time in getting started on his repeat performance of 1997. He won the Cardinals' opener against the Dodgers with a grand slam, breaking up a scoreless game, becoming the first Cardinal ever to hit a grand slam on opening day.

The legend grew even bigger as he homered in each of the Cardinals' next three games as well, tying the league record set by Willie Mays of homering in the first four games of the season. One of the homers was a 12th-inning game winner.

McGwire was proud of his early season accomplishments, but he warned still there was a long season ahead. He also was growing weary of the near-herolike status he had attained in his short stay in St. Louis.

"My theory on this is that you don't know an athlete's background," McGwire said. "You don't know where he grew up; you don't know what kind of family he came from. All of a sudden he might do something wrong, which he could have been doing his whole life, and people say, 'What a bad role model.' Maybe he wasn't a role model in the first place. Don't put that label on him."

What people should expect from professional athletes, McGwire said, is for them to work hard at their job and understand the debt they owe to the fans, the people who are paying their salaries.

"I'm realistic," McGwire said. "It's just a game. You can approach it that way if you understand that millions of kids would love to be in the situation that you're in, and that you're blessed to have the opportunity to do it. The bottom line is to have fun. I enjoy my work and I work hard."

There were no better people to second that statement than the other players in the Cardinals clubhouse, none of whom has ever been jealous of McGwire or felt he had received too much credit for what he has done.

"I've played on the same team with him, and I've played against him, and I've never heard anybody say a negative word about Mark," Stottlemyre said. "That's pretty impressive. A person of his stature in the game, because he's a star, sometimes there can be people on the same ball club or on other clubs envious of his stardom. But that's never been the case with him.

"I've never come across anybody that's said anything bad or been envious or jealous of his stardom. I think it's because he's such a great person, who truly cares about his teammates."

Brian Jordan admitted he didn't know what to expect of McGwire when he first joined the Cardinals, but he quickly found out that what you see is what you get with McGwire.

"I didn't know if he would be arrogant, conceited, or what," Jordan said. "But when I met him it became obvious this guy is a very focused baseball player. He has a good personality. I enjoy playing with him. I enjoy watching how he approaches the game. I learn from a guy like that, how focused he is, how patient he is, at the plate. He's a great example."

Make no mistake, nobody was rooting harder for

McGwire to be successful than the other 24 players in the Cardinals' locker room.

"If you're a young player, coming into this league, what better way to learn than to look out to see how Mark handles the good days, the bad days, how he handles stardom, how he handles himself off the field?" Stottlemyre said. "If you want to learn how to be a professional, he's a great guy to watch and pattern yourself after."

One young player who still was trying to get advice from McGwire was Jason Giambi, his former teammate in Oakland. They talk about once a week, with McGwire reassuring Giambi that he is going to be fine.

"If he thinks everything will be all right, then everything will be all right," Giambi said. "He never let me get down."

McGwire doesn't get down too often himself, but then it would be hard to get down on nights when you hit three homers in a game. He did it twice in the first two months of the 1998 season, hitting three at home against Arizona on April 14 and doing it again on May 19 at Philadelphia.

He became the 12th player to hit three homers in a game twice in the same season. The blasts against Arizona were made even sweeter because Matthew was in town, serving as the Cardinals batboy.

McGwire's homer on May 8 in New York was the 400th of his career, and it came in his 4,726th at-bat, making him the fastest player to reach that milestone. Ruth hit his 400th homer in his 4,854th at-bat.

Giants manager Dusty Baker gave McGwire the ultimate compliment in a game May 24. After his two-run homer tied the game in the 12th inning, Baker ordered McGwire intentionally walked with two outs and nobody on base in the 14th.

He set a Cardinals record for most homers in a month, 16, in May, breaking the record of 15 he had established in September. He set a major-league record for most homers before June 1, 25, and in less than three months broke the team record for most homers at home during the entire regular season.

"He deserves it," Stottlemyre said. "He's been a hard worker his whole career. He's been honorable on and off the field. He's put in his time. And he's one of the great players in this game. The media should be writing about him. They should be talking about him. They should be promoting him. And the reason is, he's great for the game. To me, it's not only about promoting Mark McGwire and the Cardinals. It's promoting the game of baseball and the quality of people in this game."

McGwire hit the longest homer ever measured in Busch Stadium, a 545-foot rocket off the Marlins' Livan Hernandez that hit off the *Post-Dispatch* sign in straightaway center field. The spot of impact was later marked with a giant Band-Aid.

"I was sitting on the pitch and don't think I could have hit it any better," McGwire said. "It may never happen again."

Jordan, and others, think it might.

"I'm sure none of the fans go for a hot dog when he's up," Jordan said. "Nobody moves in the dugout.

You never know what to expect. Where is he going to hit it this time? Will this be the time he hits it out of the stadium?"

At the All-Star break, McGwire's home run total had climbed to 37, equaling Reggie Jackson's mark in 1969. Starting in his 10th All-Star game, and his first for the National League, he overwhelmingly won the balloting among National Leaguers with a total of 3,377,145 votes.

McGwire doesn't believe he is doing anything differently now than he has throughout his career; he is just getting more notice and attention for it.

There were two minor points of concern early in the season—he took an unbalanced swing at a pitch in a game in San Diego and suffered spasms in his back that forced him to miss four games. With his history of back problems and other injuries, getting hurt is a real possibility and one that definitely could short-circuit a run at 60 homers.

The other was the unnatural attention his batting practice routines were receiving in the media. McGwire, primarily out of his desire to be treated as one of 25 members of a team and not as a star, didn't like people saying it was a "show" and treating his 20 or so practice swings as something more than his preparation for the game.

In Phoenix, a radio station went live from Bank One Ballpark and did play-by-play of his batting practice. McGwire called it "ridiculous." In Houston, media and television cameras were lined from dugout to dugout in the Astrodome and McGwire complained that he felt like "a caged animal" and threatened to stop taking batting practice altogether if the situation didn't improve.

Even during interleague play when he went to American League ballparks, where he has been taking BP and hitting homers for 11 years, it was like he had never been to the stadium before. At the Metrodome in Minneapolis, the Twins gave away hard hats to the first 10,000 people through the stadium gates and encouraged fans to sit in the left field stands.

McGwire also didn't like some mild criticism when it was reported that he uses the muscle-building supplement creatine. Creatine is an amino-acid derivative found naturally in fish and red meat. Doctors say they don't have enough information to judge the long-term side effects of taking creatine on a regular basis.

McGwire said creatine has helped him increase his strength while lowering his body fat.

"It's good stuff," he told the *Chicago Tribune*. "It does everything you'd want."

McGwire sees no problem with using creatine as long as the person follows the directions and doesn't abuse it.

"The only problem people have with it is when they abuse it," he told the *Tribune*. "On the back of the thing, it specifies the dosage. People think if you take 10–12 grams, you'll get big overnight. That's wrong."

McGwire's longtime friends have seen him grow from a skinny 215-pound rookie to the most feared hitter in the game. What hasn't changed is the support and encouragement he receives from everyone he knows.

"Not a lot has changed about him," said Walt Weiss. "He wants to go out and play and doesn't like all the attention. He would rather not be in the limelight. He was one of the best teammates I ever had, a guy who was positive and came to play every day, even the year he struggled in 1991. He's a special guy."

Said Tom Carroll, McGwire's former coach, "If anyone today is looking for a role model for kids you couldn't find a better one to pattern your life after. I hope he always stays that way."

Willie Stargell was a pretty good power hitter for outstanding Pittsburgh teams, but as he stood and watched McGwire along with everybody else during batting practice at Three Rivers Stadium one day, all he could do was shake his head.

"The stuff he's doing is just unheard of," Stargell said. "I've been around, seen a lot, hit some myself, but I've never seen anything like it. When he came in here last year, he hit one ball I thought was going to go all the way out of the stadium. It landed way, way up there. My mouth just dropped open."

The only person in the stadium who probably didn't have the same reaction was McGwire. That's not his style. Never has been. Never will be.

"I am here to play the game of baseball," McGwire said. "If I get a hit, a walk, or if I make a good defensive play, or if I hit a home run, so be it. If I don't, I'll just go home and think about tomorrow."

APPENDIX:

CAREER STATISTICS

MARK McGWIRE—CAREER RECORD
(Through 1997)

Year	Club	AVG.	G	AB	R	H	2B	3B	HR	RBI	BB	SO	SB
1984	Modesto	.200	16	55	7	11	3	0	1	1	8	21	0
1985	Modesto	.274	138	489	95	134	23	3	+24	+106	96	108	1
1986	Huntsville	.303	55	195	40	59	15	0	10	53	46	45	3
	Tacoma	.318	78	280	42	89	21	5	13	59	42	67	1
	Oakland	.189	18	53	10	10	1	0	3	9	4	18	0
1987	Oakland	.289	151	557	97	161	28	4	*49	118	71	131	1
1988	Oakland	.260	155	550	87	143	22	1	32	99	76	117	0
1989	Oakland	.231	143	490	74	113	17	0	33	95	83	94	1
1990	Oakland	.235	156	523	87	123	16	0	39	108	*110	116	2
1991	Oakland	.201	154	483	62	97	22	0	22	75	93	116	2
1992	Oakland	.268	139	467	87	125	22	0	42	104	90	105	0
1993	Oakland	.333	27	84	16	28	6	0	9	24	21	19	0
1994	Oakland	.252	47	135	26	34	3	0	9	25	37	40	0
1995	Oakland	.274	104	317	75	87	13	0	39	90	88	77	1
1996	Oakland	.312	130	423	104	132	21	0	*52	113	116	112	0
1997	Oakland	.284	105	366	48	104	24	0	34	81	58	98	1
	St. Louis	.253	51	174	38	44	3	0	24	42	43	61	2
A.L. Totals		.260	1329	4448	773	1157	195	5	363	941	847	1043	8
St. Louis Totals		.253	51	174	38	44	3	0	24	42	43	61	2
Major Totals		.260	1380	4622	811	1201	198	5	387	983	890	1104	10

*Led league.
+ Tied for league lead.